MEN'S SOCIETY

a guide

Social Protocol, Necessary Skills, Superior Style,
and Everything Else That Will Set You Apart from the Pack

ROCK
POINT

Brimming with creative inspiration, how-to projects, and useful
information to enrich your everyday life, Quarto Knows is a favorite
destination for those pursuing their interests and passions. Visit our
site and dig deeper with our books into your area of interest:
Quarto Creates, Quarto Cooks, Quarto Homes, Quarto Lives,
Quarto Drives, Quarto Explores, Quarto Gifts, or Quarto Kids.

First published in 2018 by Rock Point,
an imprint of The Quarto Group,
142 West 36th Street, 4th Floor,
New York, NY 10018, USA
T (212) 779-4972 F (212) 779-6058
www.QuartoKnows.com

Rock Point titles are also available at discount for retail, wholesale, promotional,
and bulk purchase. For details, contact the Special Sales Manager by email at
specialsales@quarto.com or by mail at The Quarto Group, Attn: Special Sales
Manager, 401 Second Avenue North, Suite 310, Minneapolis, MN 55401, USA.

10 9 8 7 6 5 4 3 2 1

ISBN: 978-1-63106-443-2

Editorial Director: Rage Kindelsperger
Creative Director: Merideth Harte
Interior Designer: Philip Buchanan
Managing Editor: Erin Canning
Special thanks to Johnny Chalkley

Printed in China

MIX
Paper from
responsible sources
FSC® C104723

"Make the best of every moment. We're not evolving. We're not going anywhere."

– David Bowie

Contents

Introduction

Oh, hello there! We're glad you've picked up this guide, but why have you?

A) You're looking to be an even hipper, more stylish, and more cultured man of the world

B) Someone else is hinting that you could use some "guidance" (and you secretly agree)

C) It just looked cool in the bookstore

D) Why am I holding this book?

E) All of the above

Who cares! You're reading it now, and we're here to help. Just to be clear, this guide will not tell you how to literally act like or be a man; you already know how to do that (right . . . ?!). This guide will show you how to live a better life (yes, we understand that things are already pretty good for you), including keeping your whiskers looking fine, wearing actual pants and not sweatpants, moving beyond reading *Catcher in the Rye* in high school, navigating a foreign land without being a jerk, mixing a martini just because, not manspreading/mansplaining, and much more.

First, let's establish some foundational rules to always follow:

- Be yourself. (So obvious but so true.)
- Be polite. Always. ALWAYS!
- Don't take yourself too seriously. Everyone is dealing with stuff, so a big snooze if you do this.
- Be funny. A sharp wit mixed with drollness is always appreciated.
- Don't fret over your bank account (i.e., you don't need a lot of money to have style).

Okay, now it's time to delve into the pages herein. Whether you choose to read this guide from cover to cover or to pick it up every once in a while and flip to a random page, we hope you learn a little something, have a bit of a laugh, and apply what is needed to *your* life.

Cheers!

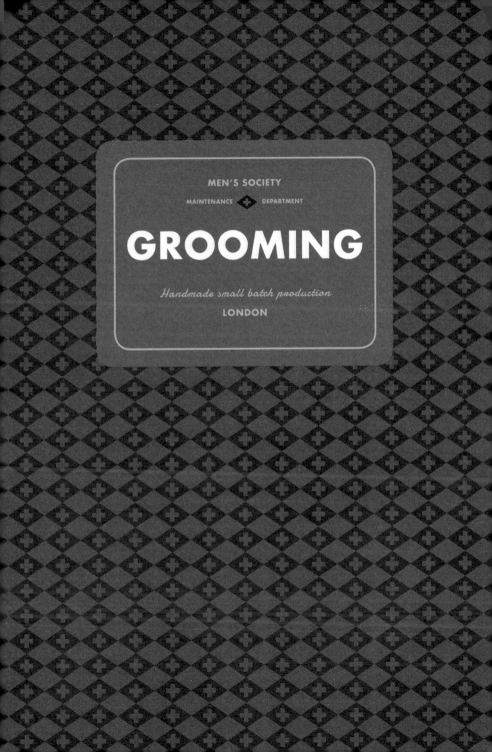

MEN'S SOCIETY

MAINTENANCE ✦ DEPARTMENT

GROOMING

Handmade small batch production

LONDON

"Fashions fade,
style is eternal."

– *Yves Saint Laurent*

CLEAN UP
YOUR ACT

T thanks to human nature, people will judge you based on the hair on your head and face. But don't let that thought stop you from expressing yourself—you can be hirsute and proud of it. In this chapter, we will help you get that hairy situation under control. Before we begin, though, let's make something abundantly clear: Proper hygiene does nine-tenths of your grooming work for you. So, if you find yourself tight on time and your options are showering and brushing your teeth or waxing your mustache, do the former.

Hair Care

A good haircut can dramatically alter your appearance. We all love a good makeover reveal, don't we? Here's how to get the right 'do for you.

YOUR STYLIST
Unless you prefer a very traditional cut, you'll want to find a hairdresser who knows how to style and is fluent in modern looks. There's nothing wrong with the cheap buzz cut, but for anything more complicated, expect to pay much more. If you're looking for a contemporary, trendy cut, the old guy in the white barber's uniform yelling at the soccer match on TV probably isn't the man for the job. Book an appointment at a shop that is recommended to you by a trusted friend or that looks like it fits your style (and has decent Yelp reviews).

ASK QUESTIONS
A haircut is like a tattoo: if you don't speak, and it ends up looking dodgy, you have only yourself to blame. Once you have found a soulmate to cut your hair, ask questions and listen. Your stylist may have some surprising insights, from suggesting you try a completely new style to advising you to part your hair on a different side. Your stylist should also know what kind of cuts will look good with your face shape and hair type. If the stylist tells you your hair is too thin for a pompadour, for instance, trust them.

HAIR TYPES
Consider what type of hair you have—straight, wavy, curly? Hair product will give you some control, but you want to work with the natural flow of your locks.

Straight hair. This type responds well to hair product and can look great molded into more dramatic shapes.

Wavy hair. This type is a gift— your hair has natural body and personality, so embrace it. Wavy hair can look great styled a bit longer.

Curly hair. Possibly the hardest to style, curly hair works well when cropped short or left longer for a wilder look.

Bald. If you are bald, congratulations! The world has taken the weight of requiring a hairstyle off your shoulders.

FACE SHAPES

Your hairstyle should fit the shape of your face, while complementing your features.

Round face. Avoid central parts and hair brushed forward onto your forehead. A short-on-the-sides, long-on-top look is usually the best way to go with a round face. Using product to give your hair some height can lengthen the appearance of your face and take some of the pinchability out of your *punum*.

HOW TO BALD GRACEFULLY

•

Balding is hard for a man to face, but there will be a point in the future when someone will see a picture of you with hair, and they will say, "Wow, you look so much better without hair!" (Whatever helps us sleep at night, right?) To avoid thinning, cotton candy–looking hair, a very short cut—such as a buzz cut—is a great option for balding men, allowing you to embrace that near cue–ball look, like Sir Patrick Stewart.

MEN'S SOCIETY

MAINTENANCE ✦ DEPARTMENT

DON'T BE *THAT* GUY

You know, the guy in a position of power who has yellow hair and a combover? THAT guy?

Heart-shaped face. Heart- or diamond-shaped faces work well with longer cuts. A more natural style using less product or products with a matte finish can help soften those hard angles.

Square face. As with heart-shaped faces, square faces work with a softer style. Avoid short, cropped cuts and straight lines, which only serve to make you look like Frankenstein.

Oval face. This shape is the most versatile when it comes to hairstyles, but like with round faces, oval-faced men should avoid central parts and heavy bangs. Though, honestly, everyone should avoid these.

BARBERSHOP TALK

You can certainly let your barber guide you when choosing a style, but knowing the exact barbershop terminology will help you communicate precisely the look you want.

Clipper numbers. Clipper numbers have a heirarchy with 5 being your conservative grandfather's cut and 1 being a skinhead's. Stick to the in-between numbers.

Tapering. Tapering refers to gradually shortening hair from the top down so the hair on top of your head is longer, and is cut shorter down the sides and back. Most modern styles—particularly shorter styles—involve some degree of tapering.

Texturing. The following terms will help you communicate to your barber what texture you're looking for, whether it's full and voluminous or thin and fine.

CHOPPED: A chopped texture gives your hair a fuller, shaggier look. Your barber achieves this by trimming your hair to different lengths at a 45-degree angle.

LAYERED: Layered hair is a bit like chopped hair, in that it is cut at different lengths; however, the effect is less choppy. Most styles involve a bit of layering, with the hair kept longer on top than on the sides and back. Layering is great for longer hair or for adding volume to thinning hair.

RAZORED: A razored texture is achieved by using a straight razor, rather than clippers or scissors, to trim length. Unlike the textures above, razoring thins the hair and allows it to lie flatter against the head. This is especially useful for men with curly hair who want to look less like they remember when disco was king.

THINNED: If you have especially thick hair, ask your barber to thin it at least every other visit. Thinning shears have teeth—like a serrated blade—that cut some strands while leaving others uncut. Thinning allows you to reduce volume without sacrificing length.

HAIRSTYLE TYPES

Certain classic and popular styles have specific names your barber will recognize. Here are some of the most common.

Buzz cut. Exactly what it sounds like—a straight, short cut using clippers. Buzz cuts are severe but convey a certain confidence. Not for the light of heart or lumpy of head.

Crew cut. Just a slightly longer buzz cut. Typically, the sides and back are cut with clippers, and the top is trimmed and layered with scissors.

Ivy League. This is essentially an even longer crew cut, and is instantly recognizable as that clean and slightly preppy style—longer on top and shorter on the sides and back. The Ivy League is less severe than the crew cut (and if the term makes you gag a little, just ask for a longer crew cut).

Caesar cut. Flat, combed-down hair with curly bangs in front. Think George Clooney in the '90s. So dreamy. Interestingly, this cut looks as charming and edgy on women as it looks ridiculous on men.

Fade. This short cut is achieved by tapering the length from top to bottom, so that the hair appears to "fade" into the skin above your ears—a "high fade"—or around your temples—a "low fade." You might also prefer a "comb-over fade." Not to be confused with the bald spot–masking technique, the comb-over fade features much longer hair on top, which is parted to the side or slicked back.

High and tight. This look requires very short, faded sides and back, usually clipped. The top is left at a medium length, about 2 inches (5 cm). This style looks great even without much product, so it is comparatively low-maintenance, but has a Forrest Gump-ish quality to it that some might want to avoid.

Undercut. The undercut is a variation of the high-and-tight look, with a bit more length. The sides and back aren't faded, but are still kept short, whereas the top is left with much more length, to be styled into a pompadour or peaks, or swept back. You'll need some mousse (page 22) handy and should be ready to match the stares this militant hairstyle will elicit.

Square. This clean-cut style requires frequent visits to the barber, as it appears uneven as it grows back in. The square cut features straight lines across the hairline, sideburns, and neckline. Essentially, this look "squares" the natural contours of your hairline for a sharp, clean look.

Asymmetrical. Just as it sounds, this look leaves the hair on one side of your scalp longer than the other. It's more modern and outré than most of the styles listed above—a bit rockabilly, a bit hipster. Embrace this look if you want something bold, young, and high energy.

Fauxhawk. A Mohawk for the squeamish.

Man bun. No comment.

YOUR HAIR AT HOME

Some men are blessed with naturally perfect hair. They can wake up, run a hand through it, and look effortless. For most of us, the "effortless" look is akin to the "head-butted a weed whacker" look. Taking a few extra minutes to style and care for your hair in the morning will be worth the confidence you feel all day long, unless you're going for that bedhead look (but that can require work too).

Find your part. Most hair has a natural part, and it's best to style with your part rather than try and fight it. Your barber can tell you which side to part your hair on (best avoid parting your hair down the center, especially if you have a round face and don't want to look like a youth pastor). To find your part, wet your hair and comb it forward. Using a comb or your fingers, brush straight up and back from the forehead, and see which side the hair on the top of your head naturally leans.

The situation. A date? A job interview? Are you going to THE club or DA club? A bolder, more styled look can convey confidence, but a natural and effortless-looking style can have its perks as well. As with all things fashion, we suggest taking the middle path—don't leave your hair as is after rolling out of bed, but try not to over-style with too much product (unless the band you're seeing that night sounds like kittens in a blender). A simple, clean, classic look is always reliable.

STYLING PRODUCTS

It might take some trial and error to find the right product, but once you do, you won't leave home without it.

Mousse. A revelation of the 1980s, mousse can add body to your hair, along with shine. Mousse is best used for hair "taming" rather than styling complicated coifs and pompadours, as the hold is relatively light. Apply to wet hair and allow to dry.

Gel. Mousse's '90s rival, gel is the way to go for a stronger hold. Apply to wet hair like mousse and allow to dry. Gel will lend lots of shine for that slick, styled look, but too much of it will make you look like a Ken doll.

Wax. Hair wax has one of the strongest holds, and will allow you to mold your hair into precise shapes. You'll only need a little—a pea-size dollop, which you can rub between your hands before working through your hair. Apply to damp hair and style.

> ### MEN'S SOCIETY
> MAINTENANCE ◆ DEPARTMENT
> ## DON'T BE *THAT GUY*
> *You know, the guy with the bad dye job, whose hair and skin color clash? Instead, be the guy who embraces his grays no matter his age.*
> *#silverfox*

Clay. Hair clay operates much like hair wax, except it leaves a dry, matte finish. If you tend to run your fingers through your hair throughout the day, use a bit of clay instead of wax, as clay has a bit more give and will look more natural when tousled. The natural matte finish that clay creates allows you to style without looking like you've applied lots of product. Similarly, dry shampoo works like clay and is good for absorbing oil in unwashed hair and for styling.

Salt water. Don't you love that "I just rode some awesome waves before work but I really didn't" look? There are several products that can replicate this effect in your bathroom: essentially combinations of salt, water, and moisturizer. Salt water will lend a bit of stiffness and texture to hair, especially when combined with a quick, cool blow-dry (go for a "sea breeze" rather than "action movie speedboat chase" look).

Hair spray. And we're not talking about John Waters right now. The prom queen of the '80s hair products, hair spray is used to set and hold whatever style you've chosen. Don't try to spray your hair and then style—you'll just wind up with a sticky mess. For a firm (and usually shinier) hold, apply spray to dry hair after using your mousse, gel, wax, etc. Then pull on your spandex pants and hit the Strip—Whitesnake's playing tonight, apparently.

MEN'S SOCIETY

MAINTENANCE ◆ DEPARTMENT

DON'T BE *THAT GUY*

You know, the guy with longer hair who thinks he's Kurt Cobain? Shampoo and conditioner are miracle workers.

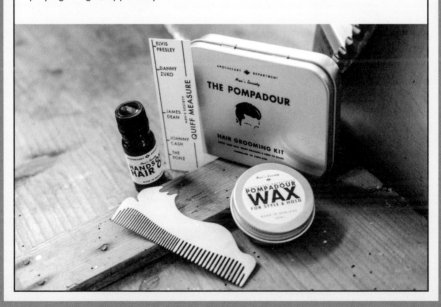

Shaving

Ah, to be young, when every shave is a journey into manhood! Sadly, this exhilaration soon wears off, and shaving becomes a chore. Perhaps that's why so many of us grow beards (page 28) these days. Chances are you know how to shave just fine; however, not all shaves are created equal. Here's how to get a smooth, close shave without razor burn.

YOUR RAZOR

Your razor choice will depend on taste, cost, and convenience. Here are your options.

Disposable razors. These razors are cheap and bare bones. Unlike fancier razors, disposable razors usually feature a single blade, no added lubricant, and no extra joints allowing the blade to pivot as it moves over your face. Although disposables will do in a pinch, they're more likely to leave you with nicks and cuts. There's a reason most hotels give them out for free. Use only in case of emergency.

Multi-blade razors. These are what you'll find in any drugstore. Unlike their disposable cousins, multi-blade razors are more durable and usually feature a strip of lubricant or gel (which wears off after multiple uses) to reduce friction and razor burn. They often have a head that pivots, allowing the blade to follow the curves of your face as you go. Despite what the package advertising may tell you, the replaceable blades on these razors usually last only two or three weeks before dulling; however, one added benefit to both disposable and multi-blade razors is that you can bring them in your airplane carry-on. Unlike . . .

Double-edged blades. Before the pivoting, gelled, tricked-out multi-blade razors came to the fore, double-edged razors were the pinnacle of shaving convenience. Handles and blades are purchased separately (when you imagine a loose razor blade, it's a blade from one of these). Unlike multi-blade razors, these blades aren't encased in a modular plastic housing, but are rather inserted into the head of your handle. These "safety razors" are very sharp, and more likely to cause nicks and cuts than drugstore brands; however, they will give you a closer shave, and a beautiful steel or chrome handle can be a worthwhile investment. The only pieces of shaving equipment that look more old-school are . . .

Straight razors. Hold up, Sweeney Todd. You probably want to leave the use of these to the pros. But if you do choose to use a straight razor, at least the blood will be on your hands, not ours!

THE SHAVE
Here's what you'll need:

Hot water
Face wash
Shaving cream
A sharp razor
Your mug

1. **Open those pores:** Before bringing a razor to your skin, ensure your pores are open and relaxed. To begin, wash your face. Use plenty of warm water. The heat will relax your skin and open your pores, which makes for a smoother shave and reduces irritation. Warm water will also soften your facial hair and lift the follicles up away from the skin, making them easier to trim.

2. **Use shaving cream:** Even if you're shaping your beard and only shaving a small patch of skin, apply cream to wherever a razor will touch your skin. Shaving cream reduces razor friction, avoiding razor burn (those raw-patterned, acne-looking bumps). If

possible, choose a shaving cream made from natural ingredients, but sensitive skin gel often works as well.

3. **Create a lather with your shaving gel or cream:** Rub it between your hands in a circular motion, and then apply liberally to your face. You want a thick lather, but there is no need to create a beard of fluffy dollops. You shouldn't be able to see your skin through the foam, but you shouldn't look like Santa Claus.

DO I NEED A SHAVING BRUSH?

If you've ever had a shave and a haircut, your barber most likely used a shaving brush to apply hot lather to your face. More than just a barbershop tradition, shaving brushes do serve a purpose. Brushes help the cream penetrate your hair follicles and lift them away from your skin (as opposed to applying cream by hand, which can inadvertently press down your facial hair). It also looks extremely cool when you catch yourself in the mirror using one.

4. **Pick up your razor and shave:** Hold your blade handle a bit like a pencil, with your index finger resting on the top of the handle to guide your stroke. Draw the blades across your face in a smooth motion. You'll want to apply a bit of pressure, but not too much. The blades will do most of the work here.

5. **Shave with the grain:** ALWAYS. Every man's face is different; however, most facial hair grows downward. Oftentimes, facial hair will "swoop" toward one or the other corner of your face, meaning your grain might run straight down on your right cheek, but more right-to-left on your neck. Feel the grain with your hand and follow it with your blade for the smoothest shave.

6. **Create a taut surface:** Stretch your skin with your free hand by placing two fingers below the jawline and pulling gently. This provides you with an easier surface across which to move your blade.

7. **Rinse regularly:** Rinse your blade under running hot water between strokes (yes, you can rinse it in a full basin, but basin water cools, and the motion of running water can help dislodge shavings from between blades). One stroke from cheekbone to lower neck ought to be sufficient, but if your razor is dull (or if your hairline runs particularly low or high), you may need to lift your blade and rinse before continuing. Avoid small, sharp strokes, as these are more likely to cause cuts. No need to rush— go slowly, especially over the curves of your chin and around your Adam's apple.

8. **Make multiple passes:** It may take more than one pass to get your skin completely clean— that's okay. If your stubble is particularly thick, you can try (gently) shaving against the grain on a second pass, or across the grain (left to right, if your hair grows down, for instance). You most likely won't need a second application of shaving cream for a second stroke, but if your face still appears stubbly after a complete shave, you can re-lather it and replace your blade if necessary. Don't forget the edges of your beard-line, either—there's nothing like finding two single long hairs on your cheekbone or neck to slowly drive you insane.

9. **Feel your face with your fingertips:** Your sense of touch will reveal any missed patches better than looking. Rinse your face with cold water to remove any excess shaving cream, and close your pores (which will help prevent clogging and blemishes). Dry with a clean towel.

AFTERSHAVE CARE

Apart from the dermatological benefits, aftershave balm feels invigorating and soothing all at once, and is a great way to end your shave. You'll find varieties made from alcohol or less-stringent versions made with aloe. Any aftershave will help close your pores, but aloe is less harsh on the skin than alcohol, and will help moisturize your skin. As with your shaving cream, simply rub a few drops between your hands, and then work gently into your facial skin.

Beard Care

Just like the perfect coif, a beard must be maintained, styled, and cared for. Letting your facial hair grow wild and woolly is not only less than stylish, it can lead to a coarse, stringy beard, dry skin, and beliefs that the end is nigh and there's a radio signal in your teeth.

BEARD STYLES

It's been said that beards are make-up for men. The right facial hair can help shape your face and hide imperfections, not to mention give you that slightly (or very) rugged look that works well with a suit or T-shirt. Similar to the right pair of eyeglasses, your beard should fit your personal style as well as the shape of your face. The key word here is balance. You want to work with the shape of your face, rather than trying to mask your features. By the same token, there's no sense in making a pointed chin pointier with a sharp goatee, or bulking up heavy jowls with woolly sideburns. Your beard should be a natural extension of your already-charming good looks.

A WORD FOR THE NATURAL MAN

•

If you're reading this guide, chances are you're looking to up your grooming game. Your grooming ritual to date might have involved splashing cold water on your face and brushing your teeth. If you haven't groomed your beard before, remember this: don't let your hair be the boss of you. Some men balk at the prospect of shaping facial hair (or any other body hair for that matter). There's nothing wrong with the natural you, but there's also nothing wrong with trimming your unibrow or shaving your cheekbones. Embrace your own personal stylized look—you (and your partner) will be glad you did.

and straightening out some of that curve. Trimming your sideburns and cheeks slightly closer than your chin and mustache will help narrow your features as well, accenting your chin.

Heart-shaped face. If you have a pointed chin and a large forehead and cheekbones, you may want to balance your features with a short, full goatee instead of a beard. You'll want to keep the hair around your chin on the thicker side, but not pointed. A pointed Van Dyke–style goatee or beard will only elongate your features (and make you look a bit like a Star Trek villain). Make sure the beard around your chin is rounded, and your sideburns are clean and short. Thick sideburns will be your face's worst nightmare.

Round face. Sick of looking like Charlie Brown? If your face is on the rounder side (which can be true for heavyset and slender men alike), consider a close cropped, rounded beard to give your face a bit more definition. Shaving higher on the neck can accentuate your jawline, squaring off your face

MEN'S SOCIETY

MAINTENANCE ✦ DEPARTMENT

DON'T BE *THAT* GUY

You know, the guy who strokes his beard when thinking, speaking, listening . . . well, while doing everything?

Square face. If you have a naturally strong jawline and accentuated cheekbones, good for you! A very close trim, or scruff, can give you that rugged look while simultaneously softening the harder lines of your face. If the all-day five o' clock shadow isn't for you, consider a full beard, trimmed close all over, rising high on the cheeks, with a clean neck. The full, short beard has the same softening effect without hiding your features behind heavy wool.

Oval face. If your face is longer than it is wide, be careful not to add too much length, especially around your chin. The five o' clock shadow may be a good way to go, though leave a bit more length in your sideburns to balance the narrowness of your face. Another option is a short, full beard, keeping the hair around your chin trimmed close. Avoid goatees and long, pointed beards.

GETTING TO KNOW YOUR BEARD

If you let your facial hair grow wild, how does it come in? Some men's beards rise higher on their cheeks than others. Some are fuller around the chin, but patchier elsewhere. Letting your beard

grow out for a few days will help reveal its character. Keeping in mind the rules for face shapes on pages XX, if your beard doesn't climb too high on your cheeks, a longer beard might suit you. If your beard naturally grows a bit thin, consider a medium-length beard, rather than stubble. Men with thin facial hair should avoid the five o'clock shadow, as stubble looks best when it's thick and even. If your facial hair grows in thick, then almost any length and cut will suit you, but be aware that your beard may come in very full. To avoid that ZZ Top look, keep it trimmed short. By the same token, if your beard grows thick and high on your cheek, lower the hairline to avoid that all-over wolfman vibe.

TRIMMING YOUR BEARD

Always trim your beard when it's dry, before washing or applying any product. Damp or oily beards can clump and clog your trimmer, making for a less even shave. Here's what you'll need:

Beard or fine-tooth comb
Beard trimmer or scissors

1. **Comb your beard:** Use a beard or fine-tooth comb to comb the hair flat with the grain.

2. **Set your trimmer to the desired length:** Remember, each brand of trimmer will use a slightly different measurement, so if this is your first time using your trimmer, start off with a longer setting (you can always trim shorter, but the idea of beard extensions makes us shudder). You can also use scissors to cut to the desired length or to just keep straggly hairs at bay.

3. **Trim against the grain:** In slow, even strokes, move your trimmer with the angles of your face, keeping the guard flush against your skin. Use very little pressure (too much pressure can force your skin between the teeth of the trimmer, leading to an uneven cut—no one wants a striped beard). You may need to make multiple passes around your chin and mustache to evenly trim the divots and dimples there.

SHAPING YOUR BEARD

The style and shape of your beard is up to you, though before you choose your shape, read the section on Beard Styles (page 28.) Chances are, the natural growth pattern of your beard is not the style you're hoping to achieve. Like a wild animal, a beard must be tamed, and though it sometimes feels a little "cosmetic" to fuss over your face too

---

TO FADE OR NOT TO FADE

•

"Fading" your beard means adjusting your clippers or trimmer so that the length of your beard is gradually shorter or longer on different parts of your face (we discuss these options a bit more in Beard Styles on page 28). You may choose to fade your neck follicles, depending on the fineness of your beard. If your hair grows particularly thick, a hard line between bushy beard and clean skin might look too abrupt.

---

much, taking a little time to shape your beard will help keep you looking stylish and neat.

The upper cheek. Most beards grow higher on the cheekbones than desired, and though I wish I could tell you otherwise, you are not Wolverine. You'll want to trim these topmost follicles for an evenly full beard. Keeping the top of your beard even can be tricky, especially as most faces aren't symmetrical. Nothing looks sillier than an asymmetrical beard, so rather than eyeballing it, use a shaving guard.

The neck. Just because the neckbeard has come to symbolize a man with three Reddit usernames and a printed pillow for a girlfriend, it doesn't mean you should shave too high on the neck. You should be able to open your mouth wide without your jawline slipping below the line of your beard. Use your Adam's apple as a guide: your beard should begin no higher than 1 inch (2.5 cm) or so above. Similarly, the sides of your beard should begin about ½ inch (13 mm) below the crook of your jawline. The line of your beard between the edge and Adam's apple may be straighter or curvier, depending on the shape of your face.

MAINTAINING YOUR BEARD

Though your beard may feel invincibly rugged, it's important to take care of the hair on your face just like you do with the hair on your head. Though facial hair is typically coarser than the hair on your scalp, you should shampoo and condition it just as regularly (if not more regularly) than the hair on your head. Even warriors polish their shields from time to time.

Moisturizing shampoo. Using a moisturizing shampoo will help soften your facial hair. Shampoo your beard whenever you wash your hair.

MEN'S SOCIETY SAYS, "RELAX"

•

Although pulling at the skin of your face can help create a taut surface that allows for a clean shave, pulling your neck skin with your fingertips can change the shape of your beard, so that when you stop pulling you're left with funny-looking lines (think of getting fitted for a suit—your tailor tells you to stand up straight, not throw your hands in the air). Instead of pulling at your skin, tilt your head back when shaving your neck. This will tighten the skin evenly, while helping to maintain the same beard shape as when your head is in its natural position.

Beard oil. If you're wondering why other fellows' beards are smooth and silky while yours is full of kinks and flyaway hairs, the answer is beard oil. Beard oil not only moisturizes and softens your beard follicles, it also works a little like a styling product, helping the follicles to lie flat against your face, avoiding that fuzzy, turn-of-the-century lumberjack look. If you plan on growing out your facial hair and live anywhere but a deserted island, consider oiling your beard an essential part of your morning routine.

ESSENTIAL BEARD-GROOMING TOOLS

Keep in mind that this is advanced beardsmanship here, and these tools are not necessary for every situation.

Beard brush. A brush not only keeps those long whiskers tamed, but it also helps rid the skin beneath your beard of any dead skin. No one wants mandruff.

The small-but-mighty beard comb. A beard, mustache, or fine-tooth comb is an essential part of your grooming kit. Like shampooing and oiling, combing helps shape and smooth your beard, eliminating kinks and tangles. Over time, combing your beard will train your hair follicles to grow in your desired direction

(to a point—don't expect to reverse the grain of your beard anytime soon). Combing your mustache sideways will prevent those follicles from hooking over your lips, which is especially important if you plan on applying those lips to someone else's in the near future.

HOW TO APPLY BEARD OIL

•

No matter the length of your beard, you should apply oil just after your shower. Squirt a few drops of the oil into your palm and rub your hands together. Work the oil into your beard, making sure to get all the way down to the skin beneath. Begin by working it against the grain, and then smooth down your beard with the flat of your palm or fingers, following the grain. If your mustache is long, you'll want to brush it sideways, away from your lips. Over time, this process will encourage your beard to grow in the direction you choose (just like styling your hair with gel or wax).

Mustache scissors. Even the most conditioned and pampered beard will occasionally sport flyaway hairs. In this instance, there's no better remedy than a good pair of mustache or beard scissors. Use your scissors to snip away pesky follicles, especially any of those aforementioned lip ticklers. (Do not use electric clippers to trim the bottom of your mustache. You want the growth here to appear natural, not cut straight across.) **Note:** Most airport security checks allow blades shorter than 4 inches (10 cm) in carry-on bags. Make sure your pair meets these guidelines before you check in.

WHAT ABOUT OTHER BODY HAIR?

Body hair can grow in some strange places, especially as we age (you see, dear reader, when a boy reaches a certain age . . .). And what you do with most of it is up to you (or your significant other), but we do have a few suggestions for the hair that may get some stares.

Nose hair. Trim it with mustache scissors. Never pluck it, and definitely don't wax it (though this seems to be a thing these days), as these methods can lead to dangerous infections. But if you do wax your nose hairs, send us videos.

Ear hair. You can trim, pluck, or wax this hair, unlike your nose hairs.

Eyebrows. The overzealous plucking of brows can go quickly from caterpillars to butterflies that have flown right off your face. If you are looking for a little shaping, go to a professional and then maintain the shape at home. If you prefer to keep them au naturel, at least tweeze to keep the unibrow at bay, trim any unruly hairs, and tame them with some wax and a brow brush.

MUSTACHE MANNERS: DON'T SUCK

•

Not just for Movember, the mustache is a bold yet legit look these days. But whether you're going for a John Waters or a Sam Elliott (we recommend somewhere in between), one thing should be remembered: consuming food, soup, or beer off your mustache is not to be done in polite company. Sure, if you're out with the guys, no one will care, but sucking Guinness foam off your mustache at a dinner party is gross. We wouldn't include this if it didn't happen so often. Use a damn napkin.

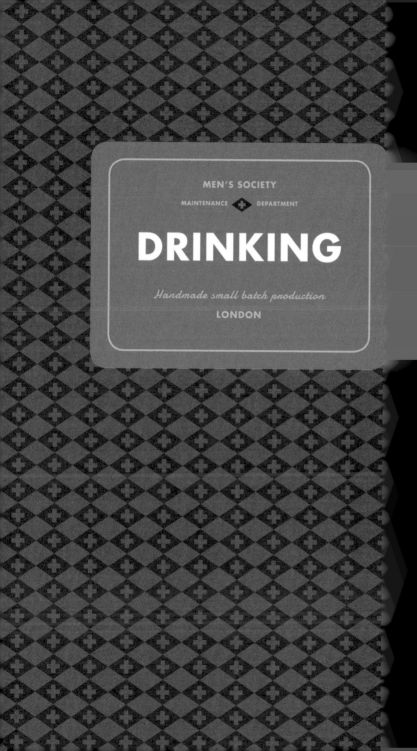

MEN'S SOCIETY

MAINTENANCE ✚ DEPARTMENT

DRINKING

Handmade small batch production

LONDON

"**Good people
drink good beer.**"

– Hunter S. Thompson

WET YOUR WHISTLE

Alcohol is a vital ingredient in socializing, enjoying fine food, and dancing to "YMCA" at weddings, but there is a fine line between having fun and getting messy. In this chapter, we encourage you to learn about and partake in spirits, wine, and beer, but we also advocate that you imbibe responsibly. Cheers!

ABSTINENCE MAKES THE HEART GROW FONDER

•

Though we include drinking in this book, we do not consider it necessary male behavior. If you don't drink— for whatever reason—it doesn't make you less of a man, and any man whose excess drinking harms himself or those he loves is lower in our esteem than one who doesn't touch the sauce. Don't let the idiots phase you—the next club soda's on us.

Stocking Your Bar

Whether it's a stylish drinks trolley or a dedicated section of kitchen counter space, every home benefits from a well-stocked bar. But rather than immediately buying multiple specialty bottles you can't pronounce, begin stocking your bar by considering both your own preferences and the types of drinks you will want to prepare for your guests. Cocktail wizardry is fun, but honestly, most folks just want a gin and tonic.

BASIC SPIRITS

Your first purchases should be basic spirits—something brown and something clear: a whiskey, and either a vodka, tequila, or gin. Gin is rarely, if ever, consumed on its own, so if you're building your bar slowly, start off with a nice vodka or tequila you and your guests can enjoy straight (and not always as a shot).

WHICH WHISKEY IS WHICH?

The term whiskey or whisky refers to a variety of brown spirits, distilled from fermented grain and typically aged in wooden barrels or casks (usually charred white oak). Most whiskeys, by definition, must be bottled at no less than 80-proof, though higher-proof varieties, such as Wild Turkey 101, are common. (A spirit's "proof" is twice the percentage of its alcohol content by volume, meaning an 80-proof whiskey contains 40 percent pure ethanol—all of which is to say, the higher the proof, the less you'll fear the police).

COCKTAIL-PARTY TALK

•

"Whiskey," spelled with an "e," is made in the United States and Ireland, while "whisky," spelled without an "e," is from Scotland, Canada, or Japan. But between us, as long as it's smooth, no one really cares what it's called or how it's spelled.

Bourbon. This is an American whiskey made with a mash consisting of 51 percent (or more) corn and aged in charred white oak casks. The high volume of sugary corn places most bourbons on the sweeter side of the whiskey spectrum.

Rye whiskey. There are two types of rye: American and Canadian. American rye must be comprised of at least 51 percent rye grain. Canadian "rye" whisky may contain any portion of rye, or none at all. Rye was especially prevalent in Prohibition America, which accounts for its presence in so many cocktails of the age, such as the old-fashioned (page XX).

Scotch whisky, or Scotch. You guessed it, Scotch comes from Scotland, and was historically made exclusively from water and malted barley. The barley is malted in peat and aged in oak barrels for at least three years, giving Scotch its distinctively earthy, or "peaty," flavor.

Single malt Scotch. This is distilled exclusively from water and malted barley, whereas a **single grain Scotch**, counterintuitively, may contain other grains in addition to barley. The word single in single malt and single grain refers to the single distillery where the whisky is made, rather than the grains used. **Blended Scotch**, on the other hand, is a combination of different Scotches from different distilleries.

Irish whiskey. Unlike with Scotch, the process for creating this whiskey rarely uses peat, so it has a smoother, less smoky flavor. Technically, whiskey must be distilled and aged in Ireland to be called Irish whiskey, and can contain a variety of malted cereals and grains. As with Scotch, a "single" malt or grain Irish whiskey originates from a single distillery, and blends are from two distilleries or more. Irish whiskey is good for driving out snakes, inspiring sing-alongs, and writing melancholy novels.

GIN AND VODKA

Though both are clear liquors, and often substituted for each other in mixed drinks, gin and vodka are different in almost every way, from production to taste.

Gin. A clear liquor primarily deriving its flavor from juniper berries, the name gin encompasses a broad range of spirits flavored with any number of fruits or botanicals. Gin comes from the Dutch *jenever*, a juniper-infused liquor that is a predecessor to the modern spirit. Perhaps the most famous gin cocktail, the gin and tonic, originated in the tropical British colonies where quinine (an ingredient in tonic water) was used to combat malaria. The addition of gin masked the bitter taste (and, we assume, the awareness of one's malaria).

Vodka. This neutral spirit is composed of water and ethanol, often distilled from fermented grains or potatoes; however, vodka can be distilled from almost any starchy or sugary plant base, even pineapple. The word vodka derives from the Slavic word for water, *voda*, but is a diminutive, meaning the more exact translation is "little water."

CAN YOU IMPROVE THE QUALITY OF CHEAP VODKA WITH A WATER FILTER?

•

This urban legend seems to be somewhat true. You can slightly improve the taste of rotgut vodka with a common household water filter. After distillation, vodka is typically filtered through activated charcoal to remove unwanted substances or toxins. Passing cheap vodka through your filter pitcher continues this process. But buyer beware: expect only a slight improvement in flavor after four or five passes through your charcoal filter, which you will then need to replace immediately.

DON'T BE *THAT* GUY

You know, the guy who eats the worm at the bottom of the mezcal bottle?

TEQUILA VS. MEZCAL

Tequila and mezcal (or mescal) are both twice-distilled spirits produced from the agave plant. Tequila is a regionally specific variety of mezcal. To be called tequila, a mezcal must be produced from the blue agave tequilana in the Mexican state of Jalisco and in specific areas of four other states. Mezcal can be produced from a wide blend and variety of agave plants, producing different flavors and character.

BASIC GLASSWARE

Every home bar should have a pair or quartet of the following types of glassware.

Old-fashioned or rocks glasses. These heavy-bottomed tumblers are essential for drinks served "neat," such as whiskey, and cocktails such as old-fashioneds and negronis.

Cocktail glasses. Any drink served "up" requires this glass. Think martinis and manhattans.

Highball glasses. For the likes of a Tom Collins, mojito, bloody Mary, or any drink that needs a mixer, this is your glass.

Shot glasses. You know what this glass is used for. Just don't use it too often.

Wine glasses. Not just for wine, this glass is "all-purpose." It is also great for serving non-alcoholic beverages, such as club soda.

BASIC BAR GEAR

In addition to glassware, there are a few essential bartender's tools you'll want within arm's reach of your spirits. Here is one place where we suggest you keep your collection small and efficient. The goal of the in-home dry bar is not to rival your favorite bar, but to equip you with the basics for entertaining and personal enjoyment. Your drinks trolley should be heavy with good times and laughs, not elaborate gear no one ever really uses.

Cocktail shaker. Include a pint glass for shaking drinks, a spoon for stirring, and a strainer for the finished product.

Bar jigger. This tool is used to measure amounts of liquor for cocktails, with a typical jigger having an ounce side and a half-ounce side.

Muddler. This is used to make any drink from a mojito to an old-fashioned. A wooden muddler is preferred by bartenders.

Wine key. Make sure it has a knife or blade attached to properly cut the foil from a wine bottle.

EXPANDING YOUR BAR
In addition to your basic spirits (page 40), stock up on more diverse liqours and mixers.

Liquor. Whether you are adding to your bar slowly or stocking up all at once, after the basic spirits and equipment, the next bottles to join your liquor family may be the following:

- **White rum**
- **Rye or Scotch** (if you've begun with bourbon)
- **Bourbon** (if you've begun with rye or Scotch)
- **Triple sec**
- **Dry vermouth**
- **Sweet vermouth**

Mixers. Choose mixers that combine well with several spirits. Many of these mixers are also best refrigerated, so positioning your bar near the kitchen isn't the worst idea. (Having a few lemons and limes on hand is key when entertaining, but we live in a world of perishable fruit, so no one's going to eat your lunch if you use bottled lemon or lime juice.)

- **Club soda**
- **Tonic water**
- **Ginger ale**
- **Cola**
- **Juices: cranberry, orange, grapefruit, pineapple, tomato**
- **Bitters**
- **Campari** and/or **Aperol**

HOW TO MAKE A MARTINI
Ah, the martini: signature drink of spies, cads, and the discerning gentleman. Mixing this most perfect cocktail is a skill every man should master. There are plenty of variations, but this is the most straightforward and classic. Here's what you'll need:

Cocktail shaker
Ice
4 ounces (120 ml) your
   favorite gin
1 ounce (30 ml) dry vermouth
Long spoon
Cocktail glass
Olives or lemon peel, for
   garnish

1. Fill your shaker with ice.

2. Add the gin and vermouth, and stir gently with the spoon for about 30 seconds (enough time to small-talk about the fact that you know how to properly make a martini!).

3. Strain into the cocktail glass.

Note: You'll notice that this martini is *stirred.* Do not, under any circumstances *shake* your martini. Though shaking is said to "dissolve" the vermouth more efficiently, the resulting drink will be cloudy with ice chips floating in it. Leave the James Bond routine for when you order champagne.

WET VS. DRY MARTINIS
•
"Dryness" refers to the amount of vermouth added to a martini, and the ratio of gin to vermouth depends on one's tastes (the less vermouth, the dryer the martini). A 4:1 gin to vermouth ratio is a fairly dry martini, though some prefer a 6:1 ratio— very dry indeed. For a truly dry martini, simply whisper "Vermouth" to your cocktail shaker before filling it with gin—this is how Winston Churchill preferred his martini.

Martini variations. You're not going to know if you prefer any of these unless you try them out. Tough job!

A **"dirty" martini** is garnished with olives, and includes an extra splash of olive juice.

A **Gibson** is garnished with a pair of cocktail onions. Note that the Gibson is a slightly old-fashioned variation, and cocktail onions are not standard in most bars. You may receive a blank stare ordering a Gibson up at a dance club during spring break.

A **perfect martini** uses equal parts sweet and dry vermouth.

Ordering a martini. Knowing your order will make the bartender's job easier, and might even impress your date. Here's how to do it right.

SPECIFY YOUR LIQUOR: Bartenders will assume you mean gin unless you specify a vodka martini, and will typically garnish with olives unless you ask for a twist (that's lemon peel, never lime). Traditionally, a martini is served "up" without ice; however, if you're a maverick who doesn't mind a slightly watery cocktail, a martini on the rocks isn't out of the question.

IS A VODKA MARTINI REALLY A MARTINI?

•

One could argue a martini is made with gin, and a vodka martini is made with vodka; however, both are perfectly acceptable, venerable cocktails. No man worth his olives will disparage your vodka martini—and neither should you his.

KNOW YOUR BRAND: Fruitier gins, such as Bombay Sapphire or Tanqueray, go well with a twist, whereas drier gins, such as Gordon's or Plymouth, complement olives or onions.

Wine

Wine is a universe unto itself. It can heighten and enrich the flavor of food, facilitate conversation, add the perfect note to the end of a long day, become a lifelong passion, and get you a little tipsy. Here's what you need to know about it.

RED VS. WHITE

Although it's true that red wine is typically produced from red, violet, or brown-skinned grapes, and white from yellow, green, or gold, it's not the fruit of the grape that determines a wine's color, but rather its skin. Red wine production uses the skin of its darker grapes, extracting both color and flavor; white wine includes no grape skins. Only the pulp inside is used in producing it.

WHAT ABOUT ROSÉ?

•

Rosé has more in common with red wine than white, in that grape skins are used in its production; however, there are not enough to produce the darker colors of red wines. Brosé, meaning when a traditionally masculine dude enjoys rosé, is a term invented by social media that should never be uttered by men who take themselves and their drinks seriously. Let us never speak of it again.

WINE TYPES: GRAPES AND REGIONS

When someone refers to the variety of a wine—say a merlot or chardonnay—they are often referring to the grape from which the wine is primarily derived. Wines are also named for the regions where they are produced. For instance, Chablis, which is made from chardonnay grapes, is a region in France (the northernmost in the Burgundy region, where much of France's wine is produced). Chianti, popularized by cannibal therapist Hannibal Lecter, refers to any wine produced within the Chianti region of Tuscany. Here are some types of red and white wines to familiarize yourself with and search for on that extensive restaurant wine list.

Reds
- **Argentina:** Malbec

- **France:** Beaujolais, Bordeaux, Burgundy, Côtes du Rhônes

- **Italy:** Barolo, Chianti

- **Spain:** Rioja

- **Multiple regions:** Cabernet Sauvignon, Merlot, Pinot Noir

Whites
- **France:** Chablis, Sancerre

- **Germany:** Gewürztraminer, Grüner Veltliner, Riesling

- **Portugal:** Vinho Verde

- **Multiple regions:** Chardonnay, Pinot Grigio, Sauvignon Blanc

HOW IMPORTANT IS VINTAGE?

•

There's much debate on the importance of a wine's vintage. In North America, for instance, growing temperatures are relatively uniform year to year, compared to Europe, so the year a particular wine is made is less important. Modern irrigation technology also makes for more uniform grape yields, diminishing the importance of a wine's vintage. Global vintage charts are produced every year by wine magazines, so if you're committed to drinking the most renowned vintages, simply do a little research before your next shopping trip. Old wine is like old art—its antiquity feels classy, but why spend more money on something you don't particularly enjoy?

VINTAGE
You may have heard wine drinkers refer to a "particularly good vintage." A wine's vintage refers to the year in which the

grapes were grown. A vintage wine is made primarily from grapes harvested in the same year. The grapes used to make most vintage wines comprise about 75 to 85 percent of that wine, depending on the laws of the region, allowing for a small percentage of grapes from other years to be used. So what makes a "good" vintage? Because weather varies from year to year, certain years yield riper grapes and therefore "better" wine. Riper grapes grow in warmer weather, whereas a colder growing season one year can yield grapes with a lower sugar content, lowering the quality of the wine.

PAIRING

The right pairing of food and wine can elevate and transform the flavor of both your dish and the wine itself. As with everything in life, this is a matter of personal taste; however, a few simple guidelines can help you make the best match. Though there are exceptions, often the color of your food will reflect the color of your wine.

- Dark red meats pair well with dark red wines.

- Lighter meats, such as chicken and pork, as well as fish, go well with white wines.

- Pair spicy foods with wines with a touch of sweetness.

- Sweet foods pair well with a light and sweet wine.

- Salty meals work well with sparkling wine.

SPARKLING WINE

•

Though Champagne, from the Champagne region of France, is the most renowned of the bubbly varieties, you can't go wrong with bringing either a bottle of prosecco (Italian sparkling wine) or cava (Spanish sparkling wine) to a festive occasion. Plus, either one is easy on the wallet!

PRICE POINT

You don't need to break the bank when buying a bottle of wine. First, consider the occasion for which you are buying it. Are you going to a dinner party where other people are also bringing wine? Are you drinking at home alone (we're not judging you) or having a casual night in with a friend? Are you tasting this wine, or crushing it?

Will Larry be there? For everything but the last situation, spend between $12 and $20 (USD) on a bottle. There are plenty of great options in this price range.

WINE GLASSES

Classic wine glasses consist of three parts: the bowl, the stem, and the foot. For the wine connoisseur, there are different styles of glasses for white, red, and sparkling wines. White wine is usually served in glasses with smaller bowls, and red wine glasses have larger bowls. The reason for these varying bowl sizes is to allow the drinker to experience a wine at its finest, including its aroma and taste. If you are just starting your wine glass collection, purchase at least four red wine glasses (for your reds and whites) and four Champagne flutes (for your sparkling wines)—the flute shape helps to preserve the bubbles.

HOW FULL SHOULD A GLASS OF WINE BE?

•

An average pour is 5 ounces— that's about five glasses in a bottle of wine—with a heavier pour at 6 ounces. If you want to truly experience the aroma and taste, you don't want a full glass. If you're drinking out of a Big Gulp cup, however, these rules do not apply.

TASTING WINE

Tasting wine is like going to the gym—no one cares how savvy or cool you look, it's about what you get out of it. There are three basic steps to wine tasting: looking, smelling, and tasting. With practice, you will develop your palate to pick out distinct aromas and flavors. Wines are often described using dozens of terms, using types of fruit (blackberry, strawberry, apple) and even terms like earth, dirt, and uric acid (yeah, buckle up).

Look. With your glass about one-third full—holding it between your thumb and forefinger near the base of the stem (always)—look

MEN'S SOCIETY

MAINTENANCE ◆ DEPARTMENT

DON'T BE *THAT* GUY

You know, the guy who orders the most expensive bottle of wine on the menu?

straight down into your glass, and then examine the wine by holding the glass to the light. Finally, tilt the glass to observe how the wine's color changes as the wine thins toward the edge. With these three steps you'll observe the wine's color, opacity, and viscosity—the wine that runs down the side of the glass is referred to as the "legs," and more viscous wines will have thicker legs.

Tip: When tilting the glass to examine the color gradients of wine, some wine tasters will hold a white piece of paper (or, if fair skinned, their forearm or wrist) to create a neutral background.

Smell. Next, smell the wine by tipping the glass at a forty-five degree angle. Feel free to bring your nose as close to the rim as possible (the key here is to smell the air inside the glass). Swirling before smelling will help aerate the wine and release its aromas.

Tip: You can clear your nose's "palate" between wines by sniffing your forearm (no joke).

Taste. Now it's time to taste. Take a small sip and hold the wine on your tongue. Rather than swishing the wine around in your mouth, inhale slightly through your mouth with

the wine on your tongue. Doing this will further aerate the wine and release more flavor. Humans taste in part through smell, so drawing air over the wine on your tongue allows you to "taste" with both your tongue and your sinus cavities. Then swallow, and take note of the wine's aftertaste. The flavor of wine will change after swallowing, as you will experience the taste "retro-nasally." Note the wine's "finish."

HOW TO TELL IF A WINE IS CORKED

When you order a bottle of wine at a restaurant, your waiter should pour a small amount of wine in your glass. Technically, this is not done so you can "try" the wine, but rather so you can smell to determine for yourself whether it is corked. However, the process of "trying" your wine first has become such common practice that sipping rather than smelling is not considered a faux pas. (Chances are, even your waiter won't know the original purpose of this gesture.) If your bottle is sealed with a cork, your wine may have been exposed to a chemical called 2,4,6-Trichloroanisole, or TCA. Wine affected by this chemical simply tastes bad and shouldn't be consumed. To determine whether your wine is corked, first smell it. Your first sniff will be the most reliable. If your wine smells musty, moldy, or like wet newspaper (or even wet dog), it is most likely corked. If it doesn't smell like something you want to drink, send it back. If you're still unsure, check the cork. If you can see lines of wine color running up the cork and reaching the top, there is a chance a pore has opened in your cork and allowed oxygen in.

SCREW CAPS
•

Bottles with screw caps are becoming increasingly more available, and aren't necessarily an indication that the wine is low quality. There are a few reasons why screw tops have become more popular, one being that cork is expensive, and cork can be poorly made, leading to corked wine (see How to Tell if a Wine is Corked, page 53). Some younger wines that don't need exposure to oxygen—unlike more full-bodied, complex wines—are also bottled with screw caps.

Beer

If any adult beverage is automatically equated with masculinity, it is beer. Spirits may be the blade with which we cut through the nonsense of everyday living, while beer is the pillow on which we rest our weary heads. But our fathers had, on average, a few brews to choose from, the modern man must deal with the craft-brewing scene, a booming beer renaissance in which every brewery sports dozens of varieties of large- and small-batch beers. If you've ever found yourself staring blankly at the chalkboard at a brewery or taproom, don't worry—the number of beer varieties available today often stuns even the most inveterate drinker.

BASIC INGREDIENTS

Though your average beer contains four distinct ingredients—water, grain, hops, and yeast—it's what brewers do with these ingredients that matters.

Water. This liquid is made of two parts hydrogen and one part oxygen. If you don't know what water is, there is a great number of books you should be reading before this one.

Grain. This is the base of the beer that gives it color and flavor. The sugars produced from the grain used in beer become the alcohol that makes beer so enjoyable. The standard grain used in beer is barley, but corn, wheat, and even rice are also used for specific brews.

Hops. These are the cone-like flowers of the hop plant; they add flavor and stability to beer, and give beer its bitterness. Brewers like to note that hops are distant relatives to cannabis, a plant we know nothing about. Promise.

Yeast. This is used to break down the sugars from the grains into alcohol. The main types of yeast are ale yeast and lager yeast (see the next section to read about what types of beer these yeasts produce).

TYPES OF BEER

Here's a quick primer on what types of beer are out there and what to look for when ordering.

Ale. Ale is slightly heavier than lager, with a darker color and a headier flavor. Ale is a broad term that technically includes beers like stouts and porters, but here are the beers that most readily identify as ales.

PALE ALE: Bready and brown with solid but not overwhelming hoppy bitterness. Example: Sierra Nevada Pale Ale

INDIA PALE ALE, OR IPA: Heavier and hoppier than a regular pale ale. Often very bitter and tough, but much loved by beer connoisseurs. Example: Lagunitas IPA

BROWN ALE: Robust and caramelly with a rich brown color and easy drinkability. Example: Newcastle Brown Ale

FARMHOUSE ALE: Refreshing bready ale with a sharp tangy flavor. Example: Great Divide Colette

FLAVORED ALE: Because it's flavorful without being overwhelming, ales are often used as the base beer for flavored beers. Popular flavored beers are pumpkin ales, Christmas ales, and fruit ales. Example: Magic Hat #9

Bitter. Despite its name, this English-style beer is actually not bitter. This beer, usually yellow to copper in color, was originally developed as an alternative to a pale ale, so it is less hoppy. Example: Boddingtons Bitter

Hefeweizen. This is a light, somewhat sweet beer made with wheat that is popular in Germany, and it's great for summer days in a beer garden. It is often garnished with orange or lemon. Example: Franziskaner

Lager. This is perhaps the most common type of beer—yellow, fizzy, slightly sweet, and easy to drink. Like ale, lager is a broad term, with considerable variation:

LIGHT OR PALE LAGER: Golden, carbonated, and sweet, and often brewed with corn. Example: Budweiser

UNFILTERED LAGER: Breadier, more flavorful, and smoother to the taste. Example: Samuel Adams Alpine Spring

DARK LAGER: Easy-drinking, but usually a little smokier in flavor. Referred to as *dunkel* at German breweries. Example: Shiner Bock

Oktoberfest. Named for the autumnal German beer festival, this rich, dark brown lager is mostly brewed in the US. Example: Paulaner Oktoberfest

Pilsner. Light, refreshing, and flavorful, pilsners are a terrific beer to drink when seeking something easy yet a little more nuanced than a lager (page 56). Example: Pilsner Urquell

Porter. A dark, smoky beer that has the winter warming qualities of a stout without as much of the heaviness. Example: Deschutes Black Butte Porter

Saison. A popular sour beer that is light and tangy yet can be powerful and heavy if consumed too quickly. Example: Dogfish Head/Victory/Stone Saison de BUFF

Stout. Dark, frothy, and flavorful, stouts are delicious and perfect for winter drinking, but can be a little heavy. Example: Guinness

IN DEFENSE OF FLAVORED BEERS

•

For every delicious flavored beer, there is a snob who will roll his eyes at you for drinking it. They will imply that your decision to drink a beer that tastes like watermelon rather than one that tastes like a burning tire is a detriment to your masculinity. But in much of the world, flavored beers are traditional during certain seasons and holidays; in Germany, some order their hefeweizen wit schuss, *meaning with fruit syrup. A real man enjoys life in all its flavors, so ignore your detractors and drink up.*

BOTTLE OR GLASS?

In certain bars or restaurants, you may be offered the chance to drink your beer straight out of the bottle or out of a glass. Two factors should be considered here: experience and temperature. If you're tasting fine beer, a glass can help open up flavors and aromas that would otherwise remain trapped in a bottle (see

Beer Glasses below). But if you're drinking a standard beer sans curiosity, temperature is king, and while some venues chill their glassware, an ice-cold bottle will keep your beer colder longer than a non-chilled glass.

BEER GLASSES

Although there's no shame in drinking a beer straight from the bottle (see Bottle or Glass? on page 57), certain brews require special glassware, beyond the pint and mug, to show off their color and retain their head. If you like lighter lagers, consider a pilsner glass. If you can't get enough of Belgian IPAs, a goblet or chalice will have you feeling like a king. Hefeweizens taste even better when served in a tall, curved Weizen glass. And dark ales, double stouts, and other big beers flourish in a snifter. Of course, all beers look good when consumed out of a lidded stein or animal horn, but we won't think less of you for using something more accessible.

BOTTLE OPENERS: THE KEY TO DRINKING SUCCESS

•

Many men's style guides will teach you how to open a bottle using things like a lighter or the edge of a table. Though these MacGyver-ish methods work in a pinch, they show a lack of forethought and class, and can result in spraying foam all over another partygoer. A bottle opener, like a watch or belt buckle, can be an excellent personal statement that lets the world know that you're ready for any beer that comes your way. While you are at it, add a beer koozie to your repertoire to be extra prepared.

Hangover "Cures"

Every piece written on hangover cures opens with the most impractical, and least useful, piece of advice: avoid drinking too much, or avoid alcohol entirely. Let's just skip that bit. If you enjoy spirits, beer, or wine, sooner or later—okay, sooner—you will get a hangover, and you will swear that you will never drink that much ever again. Liar! Metabolisms change in your late twenties, and your body's ability to process alcohol and recover quickly drops, meaning you will experience hangovers more as you get older—the same three martinis that left you feeling fresh the next morning when you were twenty-one might keep you bedridden for the better part of a day when you're forty.

WHAT CAUSES HANGOVERS?
Drinking alcohol, obviously, but the presence of alcohol in your system leads to a wide variety of symptoms associated with hangovers. Alcohol consumption dehydrates you and irritates the lining of your stomach (which can lead to nausea). It also causes your blood vessels to expand, leading to headaches, and is both an inflammatory and a depressant, causing fatigue and depression. Another cause is the presence of the chemical methanol. As your body metabolizes methanol (which is found in most spirits, along with the much friendlier ethanol), these symptoms worsen (which is why a bit of the "hair of the dog" can stave off symptoms—but more on that on page 61).

TRYING TO PREVENT A HANGOVER
Prevention is more effective than recovery, and there are measures to be taken during or just after you imbibe, and before your head begins to pound.

Pacing and hydration. Your best bet for avoiding headache and nausea the day after a night of drinking is to pace yourself and hydrate, hydrate, hydrate (with water). Depending on your size, your body will process one drink about every twenty-five minutes—drink any more rapidly and you're likely to hit the point of no return, where a hangover is almost inevitable.

Stick to clear. Bad news for bourbon lovers: brown spirits contain more toxic elements than their clear counterparts and are harder on your system. Congeners, such as methanol and tannins, are the result of the distilling and aging process used to produce the desired flavor and character of whiskey and brandy. So sticking to vodka and gin may help you avoid a nastier hangover (nastier is the key word there).

Your secret ally: ginger. One way to avoid nausea during the night is to drink cocktails with ginger. Whiskey and ginger ale is a simple combination that can settle the stomach as you drink.

THE PRESBYTERIAN

•

The recipe varies, but this cocktail is essentially a combination of ginger, soda, and bourbon, rye, or Scotch—perfect for helping you burp out that hangover belly.

Your other secret ally: pickle juice. Spend time socializing with older Russian gentlemen (which one should), and you may witness the downing of pickle juice before a night of heavy drinking. This isn't just an old folk remedy; pickle juice recharges electrolytes just as a sports drink does. Dehydration goes hand in hand with diminished electrolytes, which are the root cause of your hangover's aches, pains, and nausea. Drinking pickle juice before or during alcohol consumption can help head off these effects, and can even help cure a hangover once it has already hit. It is also a great remedy for an upset stomach the day after . . . if you can get it down.

THE MORNING AFTER
More often than not, our best efforts to prevent a rough morning fail us. Once it's too late for prevention, what is the best method for getting yourself feeling right again?

Caffeine. This can help with headaches, but the notion of using black coffee to sober up is an old wives' tale. Take it easy on the joe, as caffeine on an empty stomach can worsen nausea.

Hair of the dog? Yes, a bloody Mary can certainly make the world feel like a sunnier place for hangover sufferers. The reasons for this are many, including that your favorite morning cocktail acts as its own form of chemical pain relief, and may be alleviating symptoms of alcohol withdrawal. The hair of the dog also introduces more ethanol into your system, which delays the metabolism of methanol (which you will recall is one of those nasty congeners that create hangover symptoms). So, while not a cure per se, a bit more to drink in the morning can delay the nastier parts of your hangover until you can crawl back into bed for a post-brunch nap.

Brunch. Speaking of, drinking causes a blood sugar spike, meaning you may find yourself with low blood sugar six to eight hours after drinking. It's no surprise, then, that a heavy breakfast can alleviate some of your symptoms. The presence of food can also help absorb some of that surplus stomach acid (another reason why heavy, greasier foods seem so appealing when we drink).

Sleep. Finally, nothing quite takes the pain away like sleeping, so we recommend following your morning-after cure of choice with a long, oblivion-seeking doze.

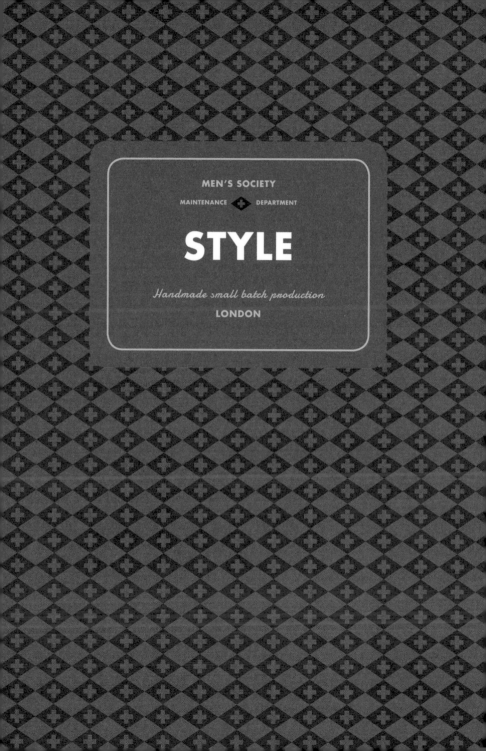

STYLE

Handmade small batch production

LONDON

"Fashion you can buy, but style you possess. The key to style is learning who you are, which takes you years. There's no how-to road map to style. It's about self-expression and, above all, attitude."

– Iris Apfel

PUT ON SOME CLOTHES

First impressions are called first impressions for a reason, and a lot of them are, unfortunately, judged by one's appearance, especially how one is dressed. That said, this doesn't mean you should dress for others; this means you should procure a personal style that makes you feel good and comfortable (not sweatpants-comfortable, George Costanza), and that reflects you. The good thing (or bad thing) about being a guy is that fashion for men isn't as trend-driven as it is for women, so you can invest in long-term pieces. The suggestions you'll find in this chapter are the mainstays that will have you stylin' for work (specifically a casual work environment), evenings, and weekends.

Wardrobe Staples

If you put a little effort into acquiring these staples, then you will come across as having effortless style. So easy!

SHIRTS

We know that you hate distracting everyone with your incredible six pack, so here are some options to keep those abs covered.

Button-ups and -downs. What's the difference? A button-down shirt has a collar that buttons (it is recommended that you always keep the collar buttoned, but if you're feeling rakish, go ahead and leave it unbuttoned. Wild!).

MEN'S SOCIETY

MAINTENANCE ◆ DEPARTMENT

DON'T BE *THAT GUY*

You know, the guy who leaves the top four buttons of his shirt unbuttoned?

Find a brand and style that fits you well—not too tight, where the buttons are gaping open, and not too loose and long. Solids, stripes, plaids; plain front or pockets—there are lots of options. More casual fabrics are usually machine washable, but check the tag. Even if the tag says you can tumble-dry, you should air-dry to help extend the shirt's life. Here's a guide to the different types of cotton shirting available.

OXFORD CLOTH: If this doesn't give you horrible flashbacks to your school days, then it's a good, classic fabric option, as it's thicker and sturdier, with a more noticeable weave, than other shirting.

POPLIN, OR BROADCLOTH: The most common shirting, poplin is thin and soft (for the man with sensitive skin) with a plain weave. It wears well, meaning there is not too much wrinkling. A wide range of patterns and colors are available in this fabric.

DENIM: Commonly referred to as denim, this fabric is actually called chambray; it has a lighter weight with a plain weave. Though most often a shade of blue, like denim, it is available in other colors and patterns.

FLANNEL: *The* fashion icon of '90s grunge, the flannel shirt is a true classic. Durable yet soft and most recognizable in plaid, flannel is a cozy cold-weather staple and comes in many colors and patterns.

T-shirts. We're predicting that your favorite item in your wardrobe is a T-shirt. We all have that favorite tee that's so old, so comfortable, and so personal. From classic white Hanes to solid-colored to cool graphic tees, as well as plain front and pocket, there are lots of options (and price points) for a dude to express himself. Regarding fit, anything seems to go these days, but if you like your tees a bit oversized, keep your bottoms slim to avoid looking dumpy. We do not recommend deep V- and scoop necks.

Polo shirts. Having gone from sporting origins to status symbol of the 1980s (it was even statusier to layer a few shirts at once), the polo shirt has now become the conservative everyday shirt for men. Snooze. But we mention it here because you can work (werk!) it if you know how. Choose a classic brand such as Lacoste or Penguin (or go logo-less, if you prefer) and a close-fitting size, then button it up. *Voilà!*

MEN'S SOCIETY

MAINTENANCE ◆ DEPARTMENT

DON'T BE *THAT GUY.*

You know, the guy who has some obscure reference on his tee that no one gets?

THE SORDID HISTORY OF THE FRED PERRY POLO SHIRT

•

A Fred Perry polo is the ideal shirt to pull off the polo shirt look, but through no fault of the company itself, it has become the uniform of fascism around the world (which the company has decried), inspired by the racist skinheads of the 1970s.

MEN'S SOCIETY

MAINTENANCE ✦ DEPARTMENT

DON'T BE *THAT* GUY

You know, the guy who wears overly distressed and designed jeans?

WHAT IS SELVEDGE DENIM?

•

Selvedge denim is produced on a shuttle loom instead of a projectile loom. Huh? In the olden days, denim was woven on shuttle looms, producing a finished edge, or "self-edge." There has been a resurgence of shuttle looms to produce jeans, but the cost of these selvedge denim jeans may be pricier because they're made in smaller batches. The way you can tell if denim is selvedge is by rolling up the bottom of the leg to look at the seam's finish, which is usually white with red thread running through it. Some people buy their selvedge jeans a little long, so they can cuff them and show off this feature.

JEANS

You can't go wrong with dark blue denim: it looks good with everything and fades well. You may even want to try raw denim jeans—denim that hasn't been washed, and is hardly ever or never washed in its lifetime—though raw denim jeans can be a commitment financially and physically. If you're feeling more rock 'n' roll, choose black or gray denim. And if you prefer a lighter blue wash, just avoid overly distressed-looking denim. Regarding cuts, stick to straight, slim, or skinny jeans—yes, skinny jeans are here to stay. Also, try to buy jeans with plain back pockets, excluding classic Levi's, of course.

PANTS

A good pair of well-fitting pants is hard to come by, as there really aren't many choices for men. But if denim is not your thing, try five-pocket pants in other fabrics (thin-wale corduroy or a lighter, cotton fabric) that have a straight or slim cut. Some workwear pants, such as Dickies Original 874, are popular as streetwear and another viable option. Plus, most workwear pants are inexpensive and durable to boot. Just make sure to style these pants in a modern way.

SWEATERS

Lamb's wool, merino, cashmere, or cotton? V-necks, crew necks, or cardigans? So many options! Fortunately, sweaters are a basic that remain classic in style and can last for years with proper care. No matter your prefernce, just make sure to buy sweaters that are large enough for layering a button-up/down shirt or T-shirt underneath without looking too bulky, yet slim enough to layer under jackets and coats.

GETTIN' THRIFTY

If you don't have the budget for new sweaters, thrift and charity stores always seem to have an abundance of them, including some cool vintage styles. Just check them closely for any moth holes and get them dry-cleaned before wearing.

SWEATSHIRTS

If you're not a fan of sweaters or have an aversion to wool, then consider the sweatshirt. Classic, crew-neck sweatshirts have been making a comeback and are great layering pieces. And the hoodie—pullover or zip-up—never goes out of style. Like with T-shirts (page 67), the fit is personal and can range from slim-fitting to a little oversize.

JACKETS

For the autumn and spring months, it's good to have a few jacket options to navigate fluctuations in temperature. You want the fit to be slim yet roomy enough for layering underneath. Consider these classic styles.

Denim jacket. You can't go wrong with a good jean jacket, preferably in a dark blue denim. But if you also have dark blue jeans, you should avoid pairing them, unless you don't mind wearing a Canadian tuxedo. Levi's Trucker jacket is a traditional style that comes in a number of blue washes, as well as black.

Bomber jacket. Derived from a military flight jacket, the modern-day bomber jacket has a slimmer fit and comes in a variety of fabrics. We suggest that you avoid leather and patches, Maverick.

Anorak, parka, or windbreaker.
Not just for rain and wind, these
water-resistant coats can come
in interesting colorways, adding
flair to any look, and are great
layering pieces, as they tend to be
a bit roomier.

MEN'S SOCIETY

MAINTENANCE ◆ DEPARTMENT

DON'T BE *THAT* GUY

*You know, the guy
who wears the collegiate
sweatshirt? (Okay, we
get it. You went to
Harvard. Sheesh.)*

WHAT ARE HERITAGE BRANDS?

•

*These are brands that have
been around for decades, even
over a century, and produce
classic, well-made pieces that
may still be manufactured
in their origin country. For
a while now, the interest in
heritage brands has been
trending, perhaps as a
response to fast fashion (trend-
driven clothes that are made
quickly and cheaply, and are
inexpensive to buy). Heritage
brands range from lower-
end Dickies and Carhartt
to high-end brands such as
Burberry. Other heritage
brands include Barbour,
Levi's, L.L. Bean, Filson,
New Balance, Champion,
Woolrich, Pendleton, Hunter,
Liberty, and many more.
And though brands such
as J.Crew and Gap are not
considered heritage, they have
been mining their archives
to bring back classic pieces
from the '80s and '90s.*

COATS

For the winter months, invest in a quality coat or two that will last for a few seasons. Here are some options for mild and cold winter days.

Denim jacket (with a sherpa lining). When you're not quite ready to commit to wearing a full-on winter coat, see Denim Jacket on page 70 and just imagine it with a sherpa lining.

Lumberjack coat. This is a classic wool zip-up coat in a large red-and-black or green-and-black check pattern known as buffalo plaid.

Peacoat. This double-breasted, navy-issued coat is timeless, whether you buy a surplus one from an army/navy store or a more modern version.

Overcoat. The ideal overcoat is a simple, well-fitted wool, cashmere, or camel-hair coat that is knee length and single- or double-breasted, and can be dressed up or down. Stick to a neutral color such as gray, black, navy, or camel. And buy a lint roller.

FASHION FAUX PAS 101

Have you ever noticed how new coats have pockets and vents sewn shut (as do blazers, sports coats, and suit jackets)? Well, the purpose of this stitching is to help the garment hold its shape while it is on the rack. But once you have purchased said item, REMOVE this stitching, unless you don't mind being judged by others as a style amateur. This also includes that little tag on the outer sleeves of coats and jackets, and any large, white basting stitches on the shoulders of suit coats. A seam ripper is a great tool for this purpose, and if you don't know what that is, ask your mother.

WHAT ELSE?

It's hard to mandate everything that should be in a man's wardrobe, so use these wardrobe staples suggestions as a general guideline, and add and delete as you like to complete *your* look. Fleeces? Meh. Shorts? If you must. Activity and outdoor clothing? Of course. Just don't make them part of your everyday look, unless your life *is* that activity.

MEN'S SOCIETY
MAINTENANCE DEPARTMENT
GENT'S SHOE POLISHING KIT
LONDON
SHOE CLEANING CLOTH
SHOE CLEANING P
MEN'S SOCIETY
NATURAL WAX POLISH
MADE IN ENGLAND
PRESS HERE TO OPEN
MEN'S SOCIETY

Accessories

Accessories don't make the man, but they can make a look. These pieces can be a true investment, as you will wear them every day, so don't beat yourself up (too much) about spending more than you expected for a pair of shoes or glasses. Just avoid trend-driven styles, because they will only last a season, if that. Also, keep it simple—someone said, "Less is more."

SHOES AND BOOTS

When buying footwear, there are decisions to be made. Do you want to invest up front in a well-made pair of leather shoes that will last you a lifetime? Or are you okay with paying less for shoes that will need to be replaced more frequently? Or maybe a combination of the two? Here are some heritage brands (page 71), with price points, to see if the shoe fits.

Alden ($$$$). Handcrafted in Massachusetts, Alden's shoes and boots are top of the line and come in numerous styles. The company offers restoration services for a fee that is much less than the original cost, when your shoes are in need of an overhaul.

Allen Edmonds ($$$). Not as exclusive as Alden, but handcrafted in Wisconsin, Allen Edmonds shoes and boots come in classic styles, and the company also offers restoration services.

Blundstone ($$). The iconic boot from this Tasmanian company combines the stylishness of a Chelsea boot with the ruggedness of an outdoor shoe.

Church's ($$$$). Renowned for making different shaped shoes for the right and left feet, Church's shoes and boots are handcrafted in England, with each pair taking eight weeks to make.

Clarks Originals ($$). At the lower end of the price spectrum, Clarks Desert Boots and Wallabees, with their crepe soles, have been adorning the feet of cool guys since the 1960s and have inspired countless imitations.

Dr. Martens ($$). With its air-cushioned sole and yellow stitching, the 8 Eye boot has been the foundation for a number of style tribes over the last forty years and remains a classic.

Frye ($$$). This iconic American boot brand continues to produce high-quality yet rugged footwear.

Grenson ($$$). The first shoe company to use the Goodyear Welt stitching technique, which is also used by a number of other shoe companies, this English brand's handcrafted shoes and boots take eight weeks to make.

Red Wing Shoes ($$$). Handcrafted in Minnesota, these work boots have gone from function to fashion to mainstay.

Tricker's ($$$$). Known for their handmade, waterproof "country" boots, this English shoemaker also offers a bespoke service.

SNEAKERS

Not only are sneakers comfortable, but they can also express one's personal style. You can't go wrong with Old Skool and Classic Vans, Stan Smiths, Chuck Taylor All Stars, New Balance 574s, and Retro Running Reeboks, but you might also want to check out these international brands. The sneaker "world" is your oyster.

- **Bensimon** (France)
- **Feiyue** (China)
- **K-Swiss Classic** (UK)
- **Lakai** (US)
- **Le Coq Sportif** (France)
- **Palladium** (France)
- **Superga** (Italy)
- **Tretorn** (Finland)
- **Veja** (France)
- **Volley** (Australia)

KEEP YOUR COBBLER IN BUSINESS

Shoe repair is a true craft, and if you have any favorite pairs of shoes that you don't think can be salvaged, think again. Cobblers are magicians, and their prices are reasonable, especially compared to buying a new pair of shoes. And if you have no repairs, stop in every now and then for a shine.

MEN'S SOCIETY
DADDY, DADDY COOL
SNEAKER CLEANING KIT
LONDON
MEN'S SOCIETY
APOTHECARY DEPARTMENT
SNEAKER CLEANING FLUID
Handmade small batch production
LONDON
MEN'S SOCIETY

EYEGLASSES

For those of you who don't want to wear contact lenses all the time or commit to laser surgery, there is the issue of choosing the right pair of glasses. Because they sit right on your face for everyone to see, glasses can make a statement about you, whether you want them to or not. And a lot of times, a style that you like may not necessarily suit your features. Here's how to navigate the world of optic frames. (Regarding sunglasses, your frame choice can be more exaggerated in size and shape.)

Consider your face shape. Is it narrow or wide? Round, oval, heart-shaped, square? Here's the ideal style to choose based on your face shape.

ROUND FACE: Look for thinner frames that are square or rectangular.

OVAL FACE: Most frame shapes work if you have this face shape. Good job, genetics!

HEART-SHAPED FACE: Look for frames that are heavier at the top than the bottom.

SQUARE FACE: Look for a rounder-shaped frame.

Be open-minded. You might have a style in mind, but when you actually try on those frames, they aren't for you. Consider all your options, because you may be surprised by something that you would have overlooked otherwise—kind of like dating.

HOW TO RESIST THE PUSHY SALESPERSON

You've made an appointment at the cute, little optical shop in your neighborhood to get your vision checked, only to be assaulted by the pushy salesperson as you exit the exam room. And $750 later, you're feeling horrible about your life choices. RESIST. Often, these people do have expertise on what looks good on one's face, and the shop may have frames that you like, but sleep on it before committing, especially if it is an extravagant purchase for you. If they don't have frames that interest you, don't be intimidated to ask for a copy of your lens prescription that you can take elsewhere.

Bring a brutally honest friend or family member. Nobody likes to hear the truth, but when it comes to this commitment—it's your face for goodness sake—it's not the time for wishy washiness. If you must go it alone, take selfies that you can share with others later. Or check out online retailers that allow you to try on frames in the comfort of your own home.

Follow trends (if you want to). The glasses frame industry is trend-driven, and it is up to you (and your budget) whether you want to be the guy with the on-trend frames or the guy who wears a more classic, signature frame. Or maybe you just want to see, dammit!

BELTS

Belts are not really required for everyday wear, unless your pants are falling down. But if you choose to wear a belt, the options are endless and a personal reflection of you (just don't wear a belt buckle shiny and big enough to see your reflection).

BAGS

Now that the leather briefcase has gone buh-bye, there are lots of great options for a man to carry around his accoutrements, including backpacks, messenger bags, satchels, and totes. Keep your bag simple in style and buy something in leather, canvas, or nylon, in a neutral color, that fits your style.

SHOW YOUR SUPPORT

Tote bags abound as giveaways at events or after donating money to a non-profit organization. If you like the organization and the design of the bag, huzzah— papa's got a brand-new bag.

MEN'S SOCIETY

MAINTENANCE ◆ DEPARTMENT

DON'T BE *THAT GUY*

You know, the guy who wears a knit hat in warm weather (and calls it a "beanie")?

HATS

A hat is a true statement maker, so wear at your own risk. Obviously, there are hats that have specific functions and should be worn in those circumstances, and baseball hats are a casual and street-style go-to. But if any other style of hat is the one you choose to wear, you're a bold man.

JEWELRY

Beyond wearing a classic watch (it doesn't have to be expensive, by the way) and a wedding ring, other types of jewelry can have personal significance. Just keep it simple.

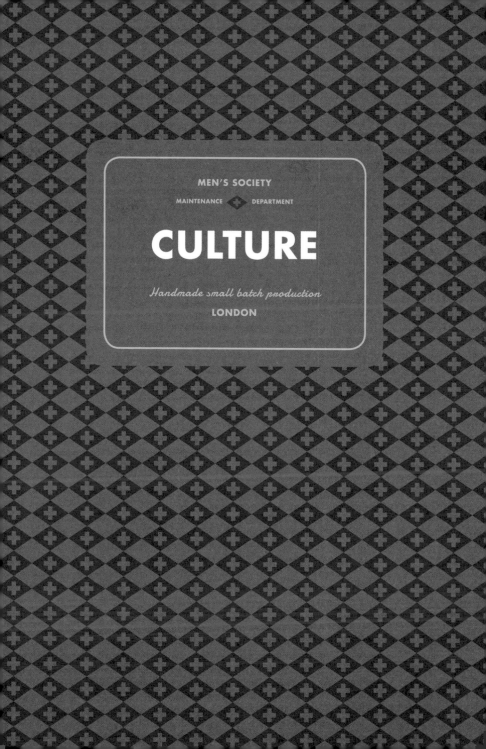

MEN'S SOCIETY

MAINTENANCE ✚ DEPARTMENT

CULTURE

Handmade small batch production

LONDON

"The only real elegance is the mind; if you've got that, the rest really comes from it."

—*Diana Vreeland*

GET EDUCATED

A knowledge and appreciation of culture, from great works of literature, to fine art and classical music, is a lifelong pursuit, and was once expected of a refined man. And those are still great things to be familiar with, as well as a sign of intelligence, but times have changed—not only has culture expanded and diversified, but it also comes in a variety of media. Like with Style (page 63), your pursuit of culture should be based on your taste and interests, no matter how obscure. You should also always have a basic understanding of what is going on in the world, including current events and pop culture. The suggestions in this section are here to inspire you, help get you out of a rut, or even spark your interest in learning more.

Books

Reading has numerous benefits, including keeping your mind sharp, so as long as you *are* reading, it really doesn't matter *what* you're reading. Of course, the literary canon is a great place to explore, but it is not the be-all and end-all of literature—life is too short to read *Moby-Dick*, if you have no desire to read, well, *Moby-Dick*. And the same goes for some modern classics. (That unread copy of *Infinite Jest* has been collecting dust on your bookshelf, right?) And though Hemingway, Fitzgerald, Updike, Roth, and Carver are all great (but also all white males), here are some additional authors and books to consider. **Note:** We have not included sci-fi and fantasy recommendations here. It's nothing personal. We promise!

LITERATURE

Here are twenty prolific authors who each have an oeuvre for you to discover, so get yourself a library card. Stat.

- **Chimamanda Ngozi Adichie (b. 1977).** Start with *Half of a Yellow Sun*.

- **James Baldwin (1924–1987).** Start with *Another Country*.

- **Michael Chabon (b. 1963).** Start with *Wonder Boys*.

- **Jennifer Egan (b. 1962).** Start with *A Visit from the Goon Squad*.

- **Christopher Isherwood (1904–1986).** Start with *The Berlin Stories*.

- **Kazuo Ishiguro (b. 1954).** Start with *The Remains of the Day*.

- **Shirley Jackson (1916–1965).** Start with *We Have Always Lived in the Castle*.

- **Jhumpa Lahiri (b. 1967).** Start with *Interpreter of Maladies*.

- **W. Somerset Maugham (1874–1965).** Start with *The Painted Veil*.

- **Cormac McCarthy (b. 1933).** Start with *The Road.*

- **Ian McEwan (b. 1948).** Start with *Enduring Love.*

- **Haruki Murakami (b. 1949).** Start with *Kafka by the Shore.*

- **Iris Murdoch (1919–1999).** Start with *The Sea, the Sea.*

- **Edna O'Brien (b. 1930).** Start with *The Country Girls.*

- **Dawn Powell (1896–1965).** Start with *The Wicked Pavilion.*

- **Jean Rhys (1890–1979).** Start with *Quartet.*

- **James Salter (1925–2015).** Start with *Last Night: Stories.*

- **George Saunders (b. 1958).** Start with *Tenth of December.*

- **W.G. Sebald (1944–2001).** Start with *Austerlitz.*

- **Zadie Smith (b. 1975).** Start with *White Teeth.*

Who Else?
- **Paul Auster** (*The New York Trilogy*)

- **Paul Bowles** (*The Sheltering Sky*)

- **Junot Díaz** (*The Brief Wondrous Life of Oscar Wao*)

- **Mary Gaitskill** (*Bad Behavior*)

- **Matthew Kneale** (*Small Crimes in an Age of Abundance*)

- **Rachel Kushner** (*The Flamethrowers*)

- **Muriel Spark** (*The Prime of Miss Jean Brodie*)

- **Donna Tartt** (*The Secret History*)

- **Amor Towles** (*Rules of Civility*)

- **Hanya Yanagihara** (*A Little Life*)

MEN'S SOCIETY

MAINTENANCE ◆ DEPARTMENT

DON'T BE *THAT* GUY

You know, the guy who read a book in high school and repeatedly mentions that it is his favorite book?

MYSTERIES AND THRILLERS
There is nothing better than delving into a good mystery, and most mystery writers have gifted us with a series to indulge in. Here are ten series to discover beyond Doyle, Christie, Hammett, and Chandler.

- **Kate Atkinson (b. 1951), Jackson Brodie series (private investigator in the UK).** The books in this series can stand alone, but we recommend reading them in order. Start with *Case Histories*.

- **Alan Furst (b. 1941), Night Soldiers series (espionage set in the 1930s through WWII).** This series should be read in order. Start with *Night Soldiers*.

- **Joseph Hansen (1923–2004), Dave Brandstetter series (insurance claims investigator in Los Angeles and first openly gay character in a mystery series).** This series should be read in order. Start with *Fadeout*.

- **Patricia Highsmith (1921–1995), Tom Ripley series (crime series featuring a con artist).** This series should be read in order. Start with *The Talented Mr. Ripley*.

- **Chester Himes (1909–1984), Coffin Ed Johnson and Grave Digger Jones series (detectives in Harlem, New York).** This series should be read in order. Start with *All Shot Up*.

- **P. D. James (1920–2014), Adam Dalgliesh series (detective chief inspector in the UK).** This series should be read in order. Start with *Cover Her Face*.

- **Ross Macdonald (1915–1983), Lew Archer series (private investigator in Los Angeles).** The books in this series can stand alone. Start with *The Galton Case*.

- **Henning Mankell (1948–2015), Kurt Wallander series (inspector in Sweden).** The books in this series can stand alone. Start with *Faceless Killers*.

- **Gregory Mcdonald (1937–2008), Fletch series (investigative reporter worldwide).** This series should be read in order. Start with *Fletch*.

- **George Simenon (1903–1989), Maigret series (inspector in France).** The books in this series can stand alone. Start with *Pietr the Latvian*.

Who else?

- **Cara Black** (Aimée Leduc series; France)

- **Sara Gran** (Claire DeWitt series; San Francisco and New Orleans)

- **Martin Limón** (Sergeant George Sueño series; South Korea)

- **Alexander McCall Smith** (The No. 1 Ladies' Detective Agency series; Botswana)

- **Olen Steinhauer** (Ruthenia Quintet series; Eastern Europe)

HOW TO FIND THE "RIGHT" BOOK

Whether you are at a bookstore or the library, finding the "right" book can be daunting. Here are a few tips to help you discover that perfect read.

Make a list. This should be an ongoing list that is easily accessible on your phone. Write down anything from recommendations by friends to books that were mentioned on a podcast—really anything that sounds interesting to you. Then consult this list when you are searching for a book to read. An app such as Goodreads is a great way to keep track of books you want to read and have read, and also what your friends are reading.

Browse the tables. Most of the tables at a bookstore display new publications, but there might also be themed tables and recommendations by store employees. Do you want to know a little publishing secret? At chain bookstores, publishers pay for certain books to be displayed on these tables. At the same time, these are often books that the publishers really believe in, so they should be decent reads.

Judge a book by its cover. What? Huh? That's right. A lot of effort goes into that design, so if you are attracted to something, pick it up. Just read all the information about the book (description, blurbs, reviews) to see if it interests you or not.

Get to know imprints. What's an "imprint"? At larger publishing houses, there are smaller consortiums of publishers known as imprints. One imprint might focus on literary fiction, another on cookbooks, and another on science fiction. Each of these imprints has their own name and logo. Look at the books on your shelves. Are there a few books from the same imprint that you really enjoyed? This isn't a fail-safe solution, but if you are familiar with an imprint's output, you most likely will appreciate other books published by them.

NONFICTION

The world of nonfiction books is incredibly diverse, allowing you to find a multitude of books on any topic. It also can be very personal, as your interests may vary wildly from your best friend's, for instance. One of the biggest compliments that can be made about a nonfiction book is that it reads like a novel. Here are ten nonfiction books (biography, memoir, music, entertainment) that read like novels and will have you learning a little something too.

- *Barbarian Days: A Surfing Life* **(2015) by William Finnegan**. A Pulitzer Prize–winning surfing memoir that catches waves around the world.

- *Basquiat: A Quick Killing in Art* **(1998) by Phoebe Hoban.** A biography of the short life of this phenom artist whose work still resonates today.

- *Between the World and Me* **(2015) by Ta-Nehisi Coates**. A critically acclaimed commentary on race in America in a letter from an African-American father to his adolescent son.

- *Down and Out in Paris and London* **(1933) by George Orwell.** The author of *1984*'s essays on experiencing poverty as commentary on this social condition.

- *Exile's Return: A Literary Odyssey of the 1920s* **(1934) by Malcolm Cowley.** A first-hand account of American writers—Ernest Hemingway, F. Scott Fitzgerald, Gertrude Stein, etc.—in 1920s Paris.

- *Just Kids* **(2010) by Patti Smith.** The memoir of the friendship between the photographer Robert Mapplethorpe and the artist Patti Smith in downtown New York City in the late 1960s and 1970s.

- *Love Goes to Buildings on Fire: Five Years in New York That Changed Music Forever* **(2011) by Will Hermes.** An exploration of five musical genres, including punk, hip-hop, and disco, that were occurring simultaneously between 1973 and 1977.

- *Please Kill Me: The Uncensored Oral History of Punk* **(1996) by Legs McNeil.** The history of punk as told by those who were there, including Iggy Pop and the Ramones.

- ***Up in the Old Hotel* (1992) by Joseph Mitchell.** A collection of essays originally published in *The New Yorker*, about the inhabitants and happenings of a New York City that doesn't exist anymore.

- ***West with the Night* (1942) by Beryl Markham.** The memoir of this English woman's experiences growing up and being the first woman to fly solo from east to west across the Atlantic Ocean.

GRAPHIC NOVELS

With its origins in comic books and Japanese manga, the world of graphic novels is thriving and one worth exploring. A lot of blockbuster movies and television shows have originated from graphic novels, and you can find a book or series on almost every subject matter. Here are few to check out.

- ***Achewood: The Great Outdoor Fight* (2008) by Chris Onstad.** The brilliantly absurd, cult-favorite comic about Ray Smuckles entry into the annual three-day Great Outdoor Fight held in Bakersfield, California.

- ***The Complete Persepolis* (2007) by Marjane Satrapi.** The coming-of-age memoir of a girl growing up during the Islamic Revolution in Iran.

- ***Hark! A Vagrant* (2011) by Kate Beaton.** A hilarious compilation of comics about history and literature.

- ***Petrograd* (2011) by Philip Gelatt and Tyler Crook.** A historically accurate spy thriller about the murder of Gregorii Rasputin during World War I.

- ***Hip Hop Family Tree* (series; 2013) by Ed Piskor.** An in-depth history of hip-hop and all of its players in comic form.

- ***Sex Criminals* (series; 2014) by Matt Fraction and Chip Zdarsky.** A bawdy romp about Suzanne and Jon, two people who happen to have the same gift—to stop time when they have sex—and who decide to use this gift to their advantage, including robbing banks.

- ***Queen & Country* (series; 2008) by Greg Rucka.** The Eisner Award–winning comic that revolves around a fictional British Secret Intelligence Service.

Music

One's choice in music is deeply personal and even emotional— a song can trigger a memory, influence your mood, and even change your life. That sounds a little dramatic, but, for instance, you might meet new friends who like the same music as you and go to the same shows. In this section, we help you discover new music and convince you why you should be listening to vinyl.

DISCOVERING NEW MUSIC
There is nothing worse than being stuck in a music rut, where favorite songs have turned to mush in your ears. Fortunately, we live in this wild technological age where music is literally at our fingertips. Here are a couple of ways to be schooled in some new (or old) tunes.

Stream it. There are lots of music-streaming options out there, such as Pandora, Spotify, Bandcamp, and Last.fm, and they are inexpensive, or even free (if you don't mind ads). Check out suggested playlists and save songs that you like. Some services even

create a weekly discovery playlist for you based on your listening patterns—there's guaranteed to be a discovery or two in there.

YouTube it. Have you ever been watching a video on YouTube, only to realize two hours later that you have fallen down a YouTube rabbit hole? Well, you might as well pick up some new jams when this happens.

Tune in to the radio. Guess what? You don't need a radio to listen to the radio! Most "real" radio stations stream online; plus, there are tons of online-only radio stations listed by genre and decade. Sometimes it's nice to hand the music programming over to someone else, and just sit back and listen, without having the ability to skip a song. This option may take a little patience, but once you find your station, you will be making all kinds of great discoveries.

Listen to music podcasts. There are a number of podcasts that focus on new music and even showcase live performances. You may even be able to download songs featured on the podcasts, for free. Try *Song of the Day* and *All Songs Considered*.

Go to shows. If you live in or near a city or college town and are a fan of indie bands, then there is most likely an inexpensive show almost every night of the week. You might also pick up some cool band T-shirts in the process.

Visit a bar with a jukebox. We're not talking about those jukeboxes that are digital and pull up any song (lame!); we're talking old-school jukeboxes (CD, or even better, ones that play 45 rpm records). If you are looking to be schooled in music from the days of yore, the patrons of these rare establishments will be your teachers. While you're there, spend some time flipping through the jukebox's pages to see what's on offer.

ENJOYING MUSIC

Duh, we know that you know how to enjoy music. But we're here to preach (preach!) to you about how to listen to music in the best way possible: on vinyl. That's right. There must be a reason why records have recently surged in popularity despite all other listening options. People swear that the sound of a record is unrivaled. So get ye a turntable or portable record player. Pronto.

The album cover art. Like with book covers, a lot of thought and effort goes into the design of album art, and the large-scale format allows us to connect with it, making the art as iconic as the music.

The ritual. There is a process that needs to happen before playing a record—the calm before the storm. The tactility of the album lends itself to the ritual of setting up vinyl to play. Here's how to do it right.

1. Choose the record you want to listen to.

2. Carefully pull the record out of the sleeve, and then remove the vinyl from the protective paper. Check that you have side one facing up.

3. Clean the vinyl by gently wiping it with a dry cloth, if needed.

MEN'S SOCIETY

MAINTENANCE ✦ DEPARTMENT

DON'T BE *THAT* GUY

You know, the guy who is a karaoke party pooper and doesn't want to participate in the fun?

4. Carefully handle the record on its sides, with the palms of your hands, to avoid fingerprints.

5. Try to line up the center hole of the record with the spindle of the turntable. This might take a couple of tries. Thank goodness for the paper around the center hole!

6. Gently lay the record on the platter.

7. Turn on the record player and slowly pick up the arm (or turn on the record player by slowly picking up the arm). Click!

8. While the record is spinning, gently place the arm as close to the outer edge of the record as possible. Don't scratch it!

9. Hold your breath . . .

10. Crackle . . . ROCK ON!

ESSENTIAL ALBUMS

Here are some classic albums you should own that will not only impress your ears, but also those who peruse your record collection. (These have all been reissued on vinyl, so you won't have to hunt them down too much.)

The B-52's by The B-52's (1979)
Yes, we all know "Love Shack," but if you truly want to shake your booty, this debut album by this band from Athens, Georgia, is an instant dance party.

The Best of Sade by Sade (1994).
That's "shah-day." Got it? When you want a little mood music and to bring it down a notch, this double-album LP has the mellowest, smoothest jams around.

Complete & Unbelievable: The Otis Redding Dictionary of Soul by Otis Redding (1966).
Otis Redding was only twenty-six when he died in a plane crash, but amazingly, he left us with a treasury of music. If you're looking for some soul, Redding serves it up on this album. "Try a Little Tenderness" will have you doing your best Duckie dance.

Enter the Wu-Tang (36 Chambers) by Wu-Tang Clan (1993). Technically two albums, this deluxe edition contains all of Wu-Tang's best tracks, which manage to be as in-your-face and hardcore as any gangsta rap, while showing off fascinating use of sample, rhyming pattern, and stream-of-consciousness pop culture references. A must for anyone who considers themselves a rap fan.

Forever Changes by Love (1967). Buy this album for "Alone Again Or," but stay for some of the finest West Coast, late '60s rock 'n' roll, led by the charismatic Arthur Lee, making this album a true cult classic.

The Good Fight by Oddisee (2015). Filled with soul- and blues-infused beats and fast, clever rhymes, *The Good Fight* is a beautiful collection of thoughtful hip-hop that inspires both personal introspection and brash attitude. A great addition to your everyday catalog that straddles the line between lively and chill, and a great introduction to what hip-hop can be for the new listener.

Greatest Hits by Al Green (1975). This is a good album to have on hand when you're feeling melancholy about romance. Al sings the truth. Check out how he's pointing at you (without a shirt on) on the album cover, probably saying, "I feel your pain, man."

Horses by Patti Smith (1975) Poet-turned-singer Patti Smith remains the epitome of downtown New York cool. The photo of the androgynous Smith on the album cover by the photographer Robert Mapplethorpe is worth the price of the album alone, but the music is legendary and one-of-a-kind, even today. To learn more about Smith and Mapplethorpe's relationship, check out *Just Kids* (page 91).

Hunky Dory by David Bowie (1971). It's Bowie, so you can't go wrong. But the four-minute track of mind blowing awesomeness that is "Life on Mars?" will stop you in your tracks. Every. Single. Time.

No Sleep 'til Hammersmith by Motörhead (1981) Sometimes, all you want is sweat and whiskey. For those moments, Motörhead's famous live album, a mélange of classics, including "Ace of Spades" and "Overkill," is a ball of speed-metal lightning that will calm the shake in no time.

Pretty in Pink Soundtrack by Various Artists (1986). John Hughes was very thoughtful about the soundtracks to his movies, and the compilation of New Wave songs on this album perfectly captures the movie and time period—and includes songs by Echo and the Bunnymen, The Smiths (Did Morrissey really agree to this?), New Order, INXS, Danny Hutton Hitters (who?!), and more.

Small Change by Tom Waits (1976). The king of the down-and-out barflies, Tom Waits's brand of seasick experimental blues possesses a world-weary soul that strikes a chord with the tipsy weirdo in all of us. Best consumed with affordable hooch after the bartender has locked the regulars in for the night.

Slanted and Enchanted by Pavement (1992). If you're looking for some true '90s indie rock, then Pavement's got you covered. Noisy yet listenable, this album had the girls and boys swooning for this band from Stockton, California. "Summer Babe" will be your anthem all year long.

Tim by The Replacements (1985). Infamous for their hard-partying antics and anarchic live shows, these bad-boy rockers from Minneapolis, Minnesota, produced some epic tunes.

ALBUM APPRECIATION 101

•

The option to skip or shuffle songs started with cassette and CD players, but really came into its own with the iPod. These functions have allowed us to override the artistry that goes into the making and production of an album. But an album is meant to be listened to in its entirety. Obviously, there are songs that are released as singles, and these are put out in the world to entice fans to the upcoming album. And once you buy the album, not every song is going to be a favorite, but there is something about listening to it in its entirety that is comforting—you always know what song is next.

Film

When discussing great films, you may be able to wax poetic about *The Life Aquatic with Steve Zissou* or *There Will Be Blood* (or *Star Wars: Episode Who Knows*), but trust us, we've heard it all before. If you're looking for a "quick" education on film history, look no further than this section. Here are some of the most influential movements in movie history, as well as a key film from that era you should absolutely check out.

GERMAN EXPRESSIONISM
Surreal, grim, and often unsettling, German Expressionism came out of the darkness of the first World War and Germany's economic decline.

The one to watch:
Nosferatu: A Symphony of Horror
(1922, dir. F. W. Murnau)

JAPAN'S GOLDEN AGE
After World War II, uncensored Japanese film experienced a golden age, with directors such as Akira Kurosawa and Yasujirō Ozu at the forefront of the medium.

The one to watch:
Seven Samurai
(1954, dir. Akira Kurosawa)

GOLDEN AGE OF HOLLYWOOD
Any "classic" American movie you can think of probably came from Hollywood's "golden age," which spanned from the 1920s through the early 1960s. From cheery and colorful musicals to rich and deeply psychological dramas, the American film industry benefited from expat filmmakers who came to the US to escape war abroad.

The one to watch:
Casablanca
(1943, dir. Michael Curtiz)

NEOREALISM
Neorealism is most famously an Italian movement. These post-WWII films tend to focus on regular people and their lives, portrayed by non-actors.

The one to watch:
The Bicycle Thief
(1949, dir. Vittorio De Sica)

NEW WAVE
This term is used to describe film movements across many cultures. The French, Japanese, Mexican, Korean, British, and Taiwanese all have some version of their own "New Wave"

cinema. Possibly the most famous is French New Wave cinema, an informal movement of French directors and filmmakers of the 1950s and 60s, including Jean-Luc Godard, Claude Chabrol, and Agnès Varda. Innovative with their jump cuts and handheld camera work, French New Wave films are also the cornerstone of cool, sleek, moody cinema.

The one to watch:
Breathless
(1960, dir. Jean-Luc Godard)

DIRECT CINEMA
Influenced by cinéma vérité in France, the filmmakers of this documentary film movement used handheld cameras to follow around their subjects for an intimate look into their lives.

The one to watch:
Don't Look Back
(1967, dir. D. A. Pennebaker)

GIALLO
Horror's classy cousin, giallo cinema uses atmospheric sets, lighting, costumes, and cinematography to add lushness to tales of dreadful murder and mayhem. Influenced by the Grand Guignol, the famed horror and suspense theater of Paris.

The one to watch:
Blood and Black Lace
(1964, dir. Mario Bava)

NEW HOLLYWOOD
Influenced by foreign films, this American movement of the 1960s and 70s features gritty aesthetics and edgy stories. Think sex, violence, and drug use. The key directors of this era were Martin Scorsese, John Cassavetes, Francis Ford Coppola, and Robert Altman.

The one to watch:
A Woman Under the Influence
(1974, dir. John Cassavetes)

NEW GERMAN CINEMA
In the 1960s and 70s, this group of young, artistic, and independent filmmakers rallied against the West German film industry to produce films that represented the current climate of Germany. Directors included Rainer Werner Fassbinder, Werner Herzog, Wim Wenders, and Margarethe von Trotta.

The one to watch:
The Lost Honor of Katharina Blum
(1975, dirs. Volker Schlöndorff and Margarethe von Trotta)

PARALLEL CINEMA
In contrast to the bright, colorful Bollywood musicals, Indian films in this movement focused on gritty realism.

The one to watch:
Rat Trap
(1982, dir. Adoor Gopalakrishnan)

CINÉMA DU LOOK

One of the most recent movements on this list, Cinéma du look evolved from the highly stylized culture of the 1980s and '90s. Perhaps to compete with television and video games, directors made their films look cool, with pop culture references woven throughout.

The one to watch:
Nikita
(1990, dir. Luc Besson)

THE CRITERION COLLECTION

•

To further your education on the best films ever made, consult the Criterion Collection's website (criterion.com). Since 1984, the Criterion Collection has made classic and contemporary films available at the highest technological standards, along with additional features. If a film is part of the Criterion Collection, you can trust that its standard is excellent on many levels.

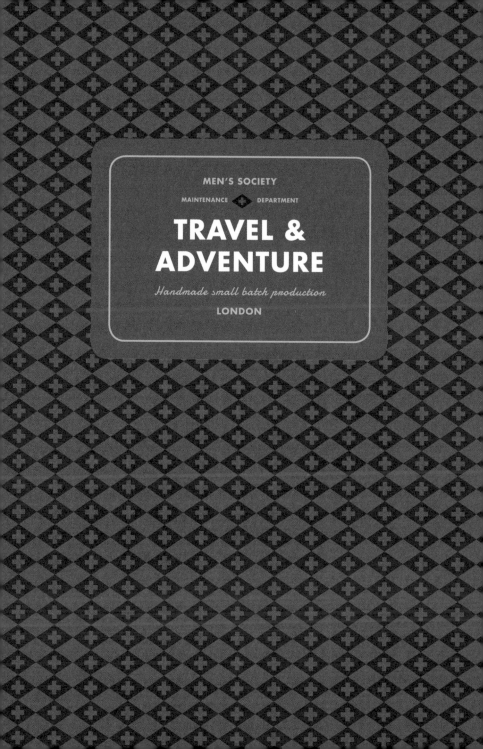

MEN'S SOCIETY

MAINTENANCE ✦ DEPARTMENT

TRAVEL &
ADVENTURE

Handmade small batch production

LONDON

"A gentleman is someone who does not what he wants to do, but what he should do."

–Haruki Murakami

GET OUT THERE

U nless something has gone terribly wrong—we warned you about using a straight razor (page 26)—you have not bled practicing the skills we've described earlier in this book (then again, we don't know your tailor). But that ends now. Clothes and barware can only take a man so far— to live a full life, a man must, at times, get out of his comfort zone. Masculinity is as much about how one acts as how one looks, and so a man should be prepared to act in the face of discomfort.

Travel

In order to see the world—or just your folks—you are going to have to travel, and most likely by airplane. Here's how to survive that tiny cabin in the sky and navigate the terrain upon arrival.

SURVIVING A FLIGHT
Whether you're a jet-setter in first class or just trying to cope with that commuter flight in coach, air travel can either be torture or a blessed retreat from life on the ground. The keys to success are your attitude and ensuring you have the proper luxuries on hand.

Comfortable yet stylish, apparel. There's no need for sweats or pajamas on an airplane. Ever. Dressing well (yet comfortably) for your flight will do wonders for your attitude, reducing that cattle-herding feeling. Also, layer. Nowhere is the temperature more manic than an airplane cabin. Bring along a thin sweater or hoodie, something you can fold and stow if need be, to avoid freezing, especially when your seat buddy turns the air on full blast.

A carry-on. Whether or not you're checking a larger bag, there's no reason to lug a heavy carry-on. Everything you will need on your flight should fit into a small backpack or, even better, a slim satchel. A small bag will be easy to stow and not take up precious legroom.

Charger. Most of us can't imagine life without our phones, especially when traveling. Bring a cord along in your carry-on for that last-minute charge in the terminal, or if your plane provides seat-side power jacks in-flight.

An actual book. Yes, your e-reader can store three thousand titles and may have wireless access and all that jazz, but rules about the use of electronic devices, and when and where they must be stowed, keep changing. Also, what if you forget the charger? Buying a book at the airport is also a good excuse to kill some time while waiting for your flight.

Sunglasses or a sleep mask. There's nothing worse than trying to doze when the guy beside you refuses to close the window shade or dim his overhead light. The solution? An eye covering for naps (or just blocking out the world for a while).

Headphones. Your personal headphones should work in most sound jacks, not to mention your phone. Make sure you have them handy for zoning to music, checking out the in-flight entertainment, or watching a movie on your personal device. Also, have you ever worn the headphones the airline provides? Ouch. Wearing headphones can also fake out that that chatty neighbor.

Money clip. After a few hours in your seat, that wallet in your back pocket will feel like a cement brick. Tuck your wallet in your carry-on before takeoff, keeping your ID and a credit card in a money clip in your pocket. You won't need cash—most in-flight beverage service is credit card only.

FLIGHT DON'TS

•

Heard of "manspreading" (page 137)? Well, the rules about it apply to flights, along with "elbowspreading." It already sucks to have to sit in a center seat, so if you are, fortunately, not in that seat, at least let that person use their armrests.

A survival kit. Pocket-size, personal cocktail-making kits abound, and what better way to treat yourself than dressing up that beverage-service gin with an artisanal tonic. And if you have a long flight or red-eye and your toiletries are in your checked bag, you may want to bring along a travel-size grooming kit in your carry-on to freshen up while waiting for your luggage.

INTERNATIONAL MAN OF . . .

No matter if you are traveling for work or pleasure and have the chance to spend some time in a foreign country you have never visited, here are some ways to make the most of your trip, experience the culture, and not go to prison. We've all seen *Midnight Express*, right? Okay, probably not . . .

Make a plan. Your plan can be loose, but it's a good idea to consult a travel guide—whether it be a physical book or an app—to get an idea as to what you would like to see and do while visiting.

MEN'S SOCIETY

MAINTENANCE ◆ DEPARTMENT

DON'T BE *THAT GUY*

You know, the guy on an airplane who sneakily uses his phone or laptop despite repeated warnings from flight attendants?

Hit the pavement. If you're in a pedestrian-friendly city, get those legs walking and/or pedaling. The best way to get to know a city and its street culture is by sightseeing on the ground. You are guaranteed to come across lots of charming restaurants and shops that the travel guide hasn't covered. And if something is too far to walk or bike to, use public transportation if you can.

Speak the language. Well, as best as you can. Your efforts will be appreciated.

Do as the Romans do. Leave your own culture behind and embrace where you are. For instance, some of the best food can be bought from street vendors. If you see locals lining up at a food stand, don't be shy about checking it out.

Keep your wits about you. No matter how internationally savvy you think you are, you will probably come across as a foreigner, so don't let your guard down too much.

Respect customs and traditions. This includes things such as wearing the appropriate clothing to visit a house of worship and taking off your shoes when entering a home in Japan.

Kids, don't do drugs. You don't want to get caught up in something that might ruin your life or even kill you. Seriously, watch *Midnight Express*. (Even in Amsterdam, don't be that tourist.)

HOW TO SAY "CHEERS" AROUND THE WORLD

In your travels, you will see amazing sites, try exotic foods, and hopefully make some new friends. There's no faster way to form a bond (even with that language barrier) than drinking with the locals. Here's how to say bottoms up around the world.

AFRIKAANS:
Gesondheid
(*Ge-sund-hate*)
Translation: Health

CHINESE (Mandarin):
Gān bēi (Gan bay)
Translation: Dry glass

CZECH:
Na zdravi (Naz-drah vi)
Translation: Cheers

DUTCH:
Proost (Prohst)
Translation: Cheers

FRENCH:
Santé (Sahn-tay)
Translation: To your health

GERMAN:
Prost (Prohst)
Translation: Cheers

GREEK:
ΥΓΕΙΑ (Yamas)
Translation: Health

HEBREW:
םייחל (Luh-kai-um)
Translation: To life

IRISH GAELIC:
Sláinte (Slawn-cha)
Translation: Health

ITALIAN:
Salute/Cin cin
(Saw-lu-tay/Chin chin)
Translation:
Health/cheers

JAPANESE:
Kanpai (Kan-pie)
Translation: Empty cup

KOREAN:
Gun bae (Gun bae)
Translation: Empty glass

LITHUANIAN:
Į sveikatą
(Ee sweh-kata)
Translation: To your health

MOLDOVAN:
Noroc (No-rock)
Translation: Luck

NORWEGIAN:
Skal (Skall)
Translation: Bowl
(Comes from the word
"skull," which Vikings used
as bowls—cool, right?)

POLISH:
Na zdrowie
(Naz-droh-vee-ay)
Translation: To your health

PORTUGUESE:
Saúde (Saw-OO-de)
Translation: Health

RUSSIAN:
Na zdorovie
(Naz-droh-vya)
Translation: To your health

SPANISH:
Salud (Sah-lud)
Translation: Health

SWEDISH:
Skål (Skol)
Translation: Cheers

THAI:
ไชโย (Chon-gow)
Translation: Cheers

VIETNAMESE:
Dô (D-jo)
Translation: Cheers

YIDDISH:
Sei gesund
(Say geh-sund)
Translation: Be healthy

Ten of the World's Best Bars

1. London
YE OLDE CHESHIRE CHEESE
145 Fleet Street, on Wine Office Court

This pub, rebuilt after the Great Fire of 1666, is renowned for its literary patrons, which have included Charles Dickens, Sir Arthur Conan Doyle, and Mark Twain. Today, anything from a multibillion-dollar deal being brokered by local investment bankers to a casual afternoon beer for Old Bailey barristers to your everyday man enjoying a drink goes down at this establishment.

2. New York
FANELLI CAFE
94 Prince Street

Since 1847, Fanelli's (far from a cafe), a former speakeasy and home to a priceless collection of boxing artwork, is New York's second-oldest bar. Perhaps not being the oldest allows this Soho establishment to be a real New York pub. There is no music or entertainment, apart from conversation with the local artists, old-school early morning drinkers, and bartenders.

3. Barcelona
EL XAMPANYET
Carrer de Montcada, 22

Located in the center of Barcelona, next to the Museu Picasso, this tapas bar has been around since 1929. Come for the cava and Catalonian food, and stay for the hospitality and atmosphere. A true hidden gem in La Ribera.

4. Amsterdam
PROEFLOKAAL ARENDSNEST
Herengracht 90

Calling all beer lovers! Serving more than 150 beers from Dutch breweries, this bar, nestled on a canal in the heart of Amsterdam, is the real deal in celebrating Holland's drinking culture.

5. Tokyo
BAR HIGH FIVE
Efflore Ginza5 Building BF, 5-4-15 Ginza, Chuo-ku

You won't be "lost in translation" at this popular cocktail bar, where the bartenders mix creative drinks based on one's tastes. Located in the basement of an office building, this hidden gem is a must-do when visiting the Ginza district in Tokyo.

6. Rio de Janeiro
BAR DO MINEIRO
Rua Paschoal
Carlos Magno, 99
Enjoy a caipirinha or two at this iconic open-air bar located in the lively Saint Teresa neighborhood. Known for its feijoada and pastéis, this is where the locals gather for drinks and conversation.

7. Antarctica
FARADAY BAR
Galindez island
Situated on the Vernadsky Research Base, this bar, the southernmost one in the world, caters to the twelve Ukrainian researchers living there, as well as some tourists during the summer months. Female travelers are rewarded with a free drink in return for their bra, which are on display for all to see. Cheeky birds.

8. Paris
LA CIGALE
120 boulevard de
Rochechouart
Easily one of Paris's finest venues, located upon the hill of Montmartre overlooking the center of the city, this unassuming music hall is horseshoe-shaped and caters to old-school Parisians. Enjoy a cigar from the tobacco shop next door and have a night to remember.

9. Helsinki
ATELJEE BAR
26 Yrjönkatu
Located at the top of the Torni hotel, this is the bar to not only get a drink, but also an excellent view of Helsinki's skyline. Ateljee Bar is also renowned for its restrooms, as the view from them cannot be rivaled.

10. YOUR GAFF
•
You might not know the lingo, but "gaff" refers to the best place in the world to drink when you don't feel like going out: your home. It's nice to stay home every once in a while and invite friends over to hang out. But make sure you are prepared first (see Stocking Your Bar on page 40 for information on how to make your home the best bar in the world).

Adventure

Perhaps the most underrated trait among men is stamina. Even the hardest punchers and quickest thinkers can be put down by an illegal low blow. So here are some scenarios that you might find yourself called on to survive—getting a tattoo, dating, and attending music festivals and stag parties. (Did you *expect* us to *expect* you to climb Mt. Everest?). Some involve the consumption of alcohol, so please review our hangover survival tips on page 59—you might want to stock up on pickle juice.

DATING

Let's face it: dating kind of . . . really sucks—especially if you are actively looking to make a real connection with someone (and not just looking to hook up). Even if you are the chillest of chill, emotions can run high, and even beyond your control, whether you have just met someone, are planning a date with someone, or on a date with someone—it can feel like there's a lot at stake. Here, we are skipping the whole how-to-meet-someone

part, as that's a book in and of itself; instead, we're going to help you get prepped and ready for that first date.

Set a date. Everyone is so busy these days, or at least they claim to be, so the hardest part of the planning might be coordinating your schedules. It is human nature to want to meet up ASAP, but patience, young grasshopper. If your potential date is having a hard time committing, don't be too pushy about it, but if they keep putting if off for at least two weeks, then it might be best to move on to your next true love.

Ask questions. Hopefully, by this point, you have already gotten a sense of your date's preferences and personality. But if not, ask questions (just don't be creepy about it). What do they like to do for fun? How do they relax? What is a typical night out?

Be a man with a plan. You have gathered your data, so now what? Dating rules have loosened over the years, which means that going out for a nice dinner isn't expected (and isn't eating with a stranger totally awkward anyway?). If you want to take some of the pressure off, plan a more casual activity, such as

meeting for a coffee or a drink, going to a concert or art opening, or doing something more active (urban exploring, pinball, bocce). Also, your date doesn't have to take place in the evening; day dates are a great option. You may also want to consider something with a finite end, such as meeting for a lunch chat where you both have to get back to the office in an hour.

KEEP IT ONE-ON-ONE

•

Remember the scene in Pretty in Pink *when Blane ("That's the name of a major appliance!") takes Andie to a rich kids' party with all of his a-hole friends? Okay, maybe not . . . Anyway, the point is, don't invite a date out on a night with the whole gang. Make it a night for just the two of you.*

SURVIVING THE BIG EVENT

The day has finally arrived, and you have been anticipating it, maybe even playing out every possible scenario in your head. You probably have a case of the jitters. These are all normal, natural responses. Here are some things you can do to help settle your nerves and not flub things up too much.

Shift your expectations into neutral. If you go into the date with high expectations, you are guaranteed to be disappointed, and if you go in with low expectations, you may bring low energy and negative vibes. Be like Goldilocks, and go in feeling "just right." Seriously, though, if you don't have any expectations, then you will either be surprised that it is going well, or not too disappointed if a love connection isn't being made.

Be yourself. Yes, this is cliché, but the more you are aware you aren't being yourself, the more you will snowball toward total disaster.

Be open and honest . . . to a point. You don't need to reveal your deepest, darkest secrets and fears, but the more honest you are, the more likely a connection will be made.

Turn it on. If you aren't a funny guy, well, um . . . good luck? But if you know you are good at making people laugh, then this is your moment in the spotlight. Good humor and a sharp wit are signs of intelligence to others, and if your date truly laughs at your jokes and self-deprecation, you are clearly connecting.

Use your conversation tactics. See page 139 for a refresher on this topic.

Don't be a control freak. Though you have planned your date agenda minute by minute, don't be a stickler if the wind changes direction. Be a team player and go with the flow. Your date will think you're a super-chill guy (and won't realize, until at least the third date, that you are true control freak!).

Prepare to pay. This might sound old school, but it's not; it's common courtesy as the inviter. If your date insists (like really insists, not a "polite" insists) on splitting the bill, see the previous point.

READING (AND SENDING) SIGNALS

We're not body-language experts here, but there are some signals that your date might be sending you physically rather than verbally. Combined with the conversation, try to take these signs with a grain of salt. Your date just might be feeling a little awkward—don't we all feel that way at times? Okay, all the time?

Body language. What we telegraph with our bodies is often unconscious, though these can be deliberate signals as well. Get a read on others and even your own body language by considering the following.

WHEN GOOD DATES GO BAD

•

If all else fails and your date turns out to be a disaster (e.g., they don't look like their photo; they ordered the steak and the lobster; there were one too many red flags), there's no reason to be a jerk about it. Wrap it up as quickly and smoothly as possible, and then get back on that horse (aka online).

ENGAGED BODY LANGUAGE:
This includes non-physical signals and the occasional physical touch, which can be an invitation to get closer. Examples include:

- Open arms
- Spread shoulders
- Hands moving while talking
- Eye contact
- Leaning in

CLOSED BODY LANGUAGE:
This is usually a defensive stance, meaning, "I don't feel comfortable here," or "Don't talk to me." The reasons a person might feel this way are countless—it's not necessarily your fault—and a shy or closed-off person might welcome you drawing them out. But notice these stances and approach accordingly. Some examples include:

- Crossed arms
- Hands on or over the face
- Legs crossed away from conversation
- Looking down or away
- Holding an object (a drink, for instance) at chest height like a shield

FIDGETING: This can be a sign of general anxiousness, or simple high energy or excitement. It can also be a sign of discomfort, telling you, "I'm not okay with how this conversation is going," or worse, "I'd like to get out of here." If your partner is fidgeting, it almost certainly means they want something to change, so be sensitive to this—try changing the topic or give them room to excuse themselves entirely. Signs include:

- Drumming fingers
- Foot tapping
- Fiddling with clothing, a pen, jewelry
- Looking away, over the shoulder, and darting eyes

Touch. Physical touch is a powerful thing, especially in situations where two people may not know each other well. As a man, it's vital to respect the physical space of others. Touching another person can be perceived as threatening, no matter your intentions, and it's important to remember that not everyone will feel comfortable enough to tell you, "Please don't do that." (Don't assume everyone is a hugger just because you are.)

> ### RESPECT YOUR OWN BOUNDARIES
>
> •
>
> *If physical touch isn't something you're comfortable with, that's okay too—shrugging or moving out of reach is a subtle way of telling that new acquaintance you don't want their hand on your arm.*

Eye contact. Like touch, eye contact can be inviting, engaging, exciting, or threatening, depending on the situation. Always make eye contact when speaking. It underscores your words, lends emphasis and urgency to what you have to say, and is a great way to let your date know, I see you and am engaged with you. Prolonged, overly intense eye contact, however, can be a bit, well, creepy. And keep the eyes up high—you know what we mean!

Flirtation and intimacy. You're feeling a good vibe with your date and are ready to make that first move, whether it be holding hands or the first kiss. But the most important thing to keep

in mind before you do anything is to TREAD LIGHTLY. Think of intimacy as an art project, where it's harder to remove elements than to thoughtfully add and build. Try to use your brain (we understand, it's hard!) to successfully navigate the situation.

Follow-up: break the rules. Dating rules are dumb. Period. If your date was a success and you're already looking forward to the next one, don't waste any time texting your dating partner, telling them what a great time you had. On the other hand, if your dating partner is texting you about what a great time they had, but you're just not feeling it, let them down nicely. Wouldn't you want someone to do that for you, rather than (unintentionally) playing with your emotions? Your date will be disappointed for a hot second. Believe us, you're not that great.

GETTING A TATTOO
Some men don't wear their hearts on their sleeves—they wear them on their skin. Tattoos have long been the chosen accessory of sailors, bikers, and Maori warriors, but lately, they have become incredibly commonplace, so much so that any modern man might find himself feeling under the gun to get one in his lifetime. But while its purpose is often to make

the wearer seem wild at heart, a tattoo is something that should be carefully considered.

BEFORE YOU GET A TATTOO:
Choose a design. For larger, more involved tattoos that will take time, effort, and money, take your time choosing something that you think will resonate with you for the rest of your life. If you like a design but are unsure about it, wait a year. Yes, a whole year—you will have the tattoo longer than that, and may grow out of your nautical phase next month. For smaller tattoos, the sky's the limit, and there is a certain old-school charm to walking in and picking a design off the parlor wall. But no matter how small, a tattoo is a tattoo, which leads to . . .

Consider placement. If you're worried about what others might think of your tattoo, abide by this simple rule: no tattoos where a court judge can see them. Pick a part of your body that can be covered by a suit. If the perception of others doesn't bother you, match the flow of a tattoo to the flow of a part of your body. A long, thin tattoo might look awkward on your pectoral muscle, just as a fat, round tattoo might appear clumsy on your forearm. Think of arrows flowing around the shape of your body—let the tattoo move along them.

PAIN TOLERANCE
•
There is no such thing as a painless tattoo, so if pain bothers you, choose a part of the body that is meaty and far from a nerve cluster. The arm, shoulder, and thigh isn't terrible, but stomach, tailbone, hand, and head tattoos can be brutal.

Choose an artist and a parlor. If your tattoo is simple and small, most artists will be able to grind it out. But if you're looking for something more nuanced, research artists so you can find someone whose style and skill matches what you're looking for. Then schedule a consultation so you can discuss your ideas with them. Bedside manner is important, especially when you intend to pay this person to hurt you for over an hour. While there, observe their parlor. Does it look clean? Is everyone cordial and professional?

Agree on a price. You can't return a tattoo once you discover that it costs twice as much as you expected. During your consultation, make sure to ask how much they think the tattoo will cost. If it's too much, talk to your artist, but don't wheel and deal with them.

WHEN GETTING YOUR TATTOO:

Show up on time and sober. Tattoo artists may seem cool and aloof, but this is their job, and showing up late can throw off their day's schedule. On top of that, do not attempt to prepare yourself for the pain of getting tattooed with drink and drugs; the former thins the blood, meaning you will ooze all over the place while being inked, and the latter can cause you to faint, throw up, or worse. If you're not ready to come in, sit down, and do this, then you should most likely wait to get a tattoo.

Get sizing and placement right. Seconds before the first scratch of the needle is not the time to decide that your tattoo is too big and should be a few inches farther down. Your artist will create an ink stencil that they will then stick to your body and peel away so that the design remains (sort of like a temporary tattoo). Feel free to ask your artist to make it smaller, or to wipe off the stencil and place it somewhere else. A good artist will comply, though you should probably not ask them to change it more than four times.

Don't freak out at the sound. A tattoo gun is a machine that moves a needle up and down about three thousand times per minute. It is meant to sound like a giant robotic hornet. Calm down.

Hold still. Tattoos hurt—that's sort of the point. So, when you first get zapped, don't flinch, lest that eagle ends up looking like a flamingo. Feel free to express the pain to your artist; some tattoo artists even enjoy small talk while doing their job.

AFTER GETTING YOUR TATTOO:

Pay and tip. Good work deserves a little something extra. Pay your artist, preferably in cash, and tip them for their time and trouble. How much you tip is up to you, but 20 to 25 percent is the standard, especially if your tattoo is well done. Doing this will also help get you preferential treatment if you return for another one.

Leave it alone for twelve to twenty-four hours. Once they have finished, your tattoo artist will bandage your new tattoo. The tattoo will then bleed and ooze a little ink, so give it time. You may want to peel off the bandage and show your friends at the bar, but be patient—messing with a tattoo too early could cause infection.

The first three days: wash and use ointment. For the first three days, gently hand-wash your tattoo with warm water and unscented antibacterial soap three times a day. Do not use washcloths, loofahs, or anything else that might scrape away your healing skin. Then pat it dry and gently rub a thin layer of A&D ointment (do not use ointments such as NEOSPORIN or Bactine—simple A&D ointment) over the tattoo.

The next ten days: moisturize, don't stretch. On day four, replace the A&D ointment with simple unscented lotion. During this time, your tattoo will flake and peel, which is natural. It will also itch like hell, but whatever you do, don't scratch it, or you'll chip away at ink-imbued skin. Instead, slapping your tattoo will help ease the itch. Meanwhile, avoid exercises that will stretch the area where you've just been inked (for instance, if you have a chest tattoo, skip the bench press).

The next six months: no sun, no swimming. Chlorine, saltwater, and exposure to sun will all cause your tattoo to fade prematurely. Take it easy and keep your tattoo out of the sun and water.

TATTOOS YOU SHOULD NEVER GET

A tattoo is your choice and yours alone. But take it from us: the following tattoo ideas have never been good ones.

Something in a language you don't speak. You may find the Korean alphabet to be very beautiful, and your birthright trip may have given you a deep love of Hebrew, but unless you can read your own tattoo, there is a great chance it will say, "A FOOL AND HIS MONEY ARE SOON PARTED."

Symbols of a religion you don't practice. Similar to the previous point, your fascination with Kabbalah or voodoo will not charm someone who has dedicated their life to practicing that faith.

Political symbols or slogans. You may no longer love a specific band or cartoon character, but at least their logo or image will remind you of who you once were. Altered beliefs, on the other hand, are not often the source of much nostalgia.

Tribal. Unless you are an ultimate fighter, you should not get a tribal tattoo.

SURVIVING A MUSIC FESTIVAL

Ah, the multiday, outdoor music festival—a tradition even the most proper gentleman should try at least once in his life. But while these raucous events are full of spontaneous magic and hilarious debauchery, they also include overflowing porta potties and mile-long lines for alcohol. Here are some things to consider when planning a trip to Bonaroo, Wacken, Glastonbury, and beyond.

Splurge on accommodations. Given how expensive tickets, travel, food, and drink can be, it's totally understandable that you want to bargain hunt for your accommodations. But money will seem like a foolish concern when rain begins to pour through your tent. Do you really think everyone who attended Woodstock loved the rain?

Wear comfortable shoes. Most music festivals involve standing for long stretches of time while watching your favorite band (or waiting for them to show up). Comfortable shoes or a pair of insoles will help keep your dogs from barking.

Stay hydrated. Nothing will crush your appearance and stamina like dehydration. Drinking water between each adult beverage will help keep you spry and (somewhat) lucid for the long haul.

Keep your wits about you. We're no angels—at a music festival, you might drink a random green rum concoction or smoke a funny-smelling cigarette. But losing your wallet, tent, and mind, surrounded by thousands of people is no fun, and a bad look all around, so stick to the lightweight substances.

UH, WHERE DID I PARK?

•

It's bad enough trying to find your car in the parking lot at IKEA, but imagine not remembering where you parked while utterly exhausted and badly in need of a shower. Take photos and make notes, and have your buddies do the same so you have backup information.

MEN'S SOCIETY
SURVIVAL
DEPARTMENT
THE FESTIVAL
URVIVAL KIT
LONDON
MEN'S SOCIETY
SURVIVAL DEPARTMENT
THE PONCHO
MARVIS
10ml e NET WT. 0.5 oz
MEN'S SOCIETY
1. Can Op
2. Knife ed
3. Screwdriv
4. Ruler
5. Bottle Open
6. Four
7. Butter
8. Saw B
9. Directi
Indicat
10. Two
11. Keyri

Loose lips can ruin trips.
Why is that dreadlocked Swede you bummed a smoke from so interested in where your tent is? If you get a bad feeling, or even a weird feeling, about someone you don't know, it is best to keep where you're sleeping and what you have on you to yourself.

Wear earplugs. You may consider yourself a tough customer, but even the guys onstage are wearing earplugs. Bring a pair of soft foam plugs so that this won't be the last concert, or music festival, you enjoy.

Cover up. You know what's not a good look? Sun poisoning. Slap on plenty of sunscreen, even if the weather is overcast (applying every couple of hours, especially if you sweat a lot). And wear a hat. This is your chance to finally let your true hat personality shine (see page 81).

SURVIVING THE ALL-GUY PARTY WEEKEND

No matter how put together and practiced you are, reader, you have that one friend. You know the one—the guy with a heart of gold and a sewer for a mind, whose name makes your significant other shake their head in contempt. Eventually, that friend will get

promoted, propose to his long-term partner, or make bail, and it is your duty, as a man, to throw him a weekend-long party that would make your mother gasp. We're not here to tell you how to throw that bacchanal (there are other books for that) but we will tell you how to make it through this weekend looking and feeling good (or at least not terrible).

Budget, budget, budget. Two-and-a-half days of mayhem require a ready-for-anything attitude, but no one likes coming home to find someone repossessing their car. Before you venture into the unknown, take a moment to plan out your personal budget, taking meals, accommodations, and travel into account.

Stirred, not sugary. Hand grenades may be a New Orleans tradition, but so is waking up hugging a toilet. Sugary-sweet drinks go right to your head, taking you from zero to "let's play tag with Roman candles" (please don't do this!) in an instant. Keep your drinks simple, pace yourself, and sip a glass of water in between.

> ### "LIQUOR BEFORE BEER NEVER FEAR" OR "BEER BEFORE LIQUOR NEVER SICKER"?
>
> •
>
> *Which rule is correct? Neither of them. Alcohol is alcohol. So, follow this rule:* **TRY NOT TO OVERDO IT!**

Shower when you can. Because you're partying with one or more fellow men, you might become desensitized to just how much like a gym bag you smell. So, when everyone takes a brief break (or are passed out), don't use that time to flip channels or wander the hotel—hop in the shower. Your inner gentleman, and everyone around you, will thank you.

Eat healthy-ish. A couple of greasy burgers might sound like the ultimate hangover cure, and that's fine if you have the whole day to sleep it off, but hold off on the gorging if there is another day of activities. You will only feel bloated, tired, and unable to party. Eat something that can soak up the previous night's liquor, but isn't too heavy.

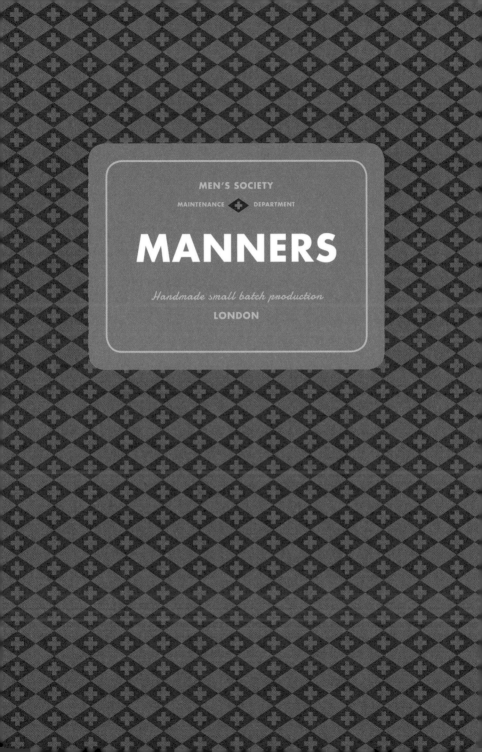

"The greatness of a man is not in how much wealth he acquires, but in his integrity and his ability to affect those around him positively."

–Bob Marley

TURN ON THE CHARM

D) o you remember the scene in the movie *Singles* when Bridget Fonda's character is describing what she's looking for in a man? (Oh, right, you were born in 1996 . . .) Anyway, she says that she wants "someone who said 'bless you' or 'gesundheit'" when she sneezed. It's that simple. That's all it takes to be polite. The world is depending on gentlemen like you, yes YOU, to keep these traditions alive. We're not talking about knowing the ins and outs of using a finger bowl at a dinner party; these are simple courtesies that are guaranteed to brighten your and someone else's day. Gesundheit!

Public Etiquette

The inhabitants of this busy world we're living in seem to be growing ruder by the minute. But that doesn't mean you have to play by these new rules. And if you're civilized in your everyday interactions, others may even take notice and learn a thing or two.

COMMON COURTESIES

If you aren't already practicing most of these things, then it's going to be hard for us to be friends. (And we were getting along so well up to this point.)

Use your words. There are only four words/phrases that you need to utter—outside of normal communication, that is—to comfortably make it through your day: please, thank-you, excuse me, and you're welcome. (And the fourth one is usually in response to you being polite in the first place. Imagine that!) Add a smile with your words, and your recipient will be religiously checking the Missed Connections section of Craigslist.

Open doors. If you are the first one to reach a door and there is anyone in the vicinity of either side of it, HOLD. IT. OPEN. PERIOD.

COURTESY: WOMEN VS. MEN
•
Many of the tips in this section— holding doors, giving up a seat on public transportation, and so on—have a kind of chivalry when performed to accommodate women. And certain men will argue that acts of courtesy toward women is somehow a form of sexism. If women want to be treated the same as men, these men whine, "Then they should hold their own damn doors."

And to be fair, women don't always need your courtesy, and they will survive without it. But that's the point of courtesy—you just do it because it's nice, and because the world shouldn't operate according to the law of the jungle. At the end of the day wouldn't you rather be considered a gentleman than some jerk?

Walk the walk. There is nothing more annoying than getting stuck behind someone who is doing an incredible job at taking up the entire sidewalk, all by themselves. So, stick to the proper side of traffic flow, and put your phone away—your Instagram feed isn't going anywhere. If you must talk or text, move to an area where you are out of the way.

PUBLIC TRANSPORTATION

It is already a struggle just to get up and ready for work, so no one needs their day ruined, first thing, by some jerk on a crowded train or bus.

Stand. If you are an able-bodied man, you don't need to fight ladies (of all ages), elderly men, and those who are disabled for a seat. Stand, unless . . .

Sit. If there are plenty of empty seats, sit down, but be prepared to give it up once the train or bus grows more crowded.

What else? Here are some additional things you can do to make your and others' ride extra smooth:

- Move into the train/bus instead of blocking the door.

- Scooch to the inside seat of a pair of side-by-side seats.

- Place your backpack (of any size) on one shoulder and hold it in front of you.

MANSPREADING

•

This is a derogatory term that you don't want used to describe you. Do you really need a foot (or more) of space between your legs when sitting, or to lean your elbows on your knees, encroaching upon a second seat? All the ladies on the train will be giving you the stink-eye and thinking, "I can't believe that guy is actually someone's husband/partner/son/father." Okay, maybe just one woman, but you're now going to think twice about manspreading, right?

SOCIAL SITUATIONS

Whether you are socializing with good friends, work colleagues, or new acquaintances, there's an unspoken code on how to "treat" one another. You don't want to be known as a freeloader.

Reciprocate. If someone buys you a drink, make sure to get them a drink next round, or the next time you go out. Heck, offer to buy the first round, and if your friends and colleagues are courteous like you, they should return the favor. The same rule applies when someone buys you a meal.

Be generous if, and when, you can. Social situations can get tricky, especially when the people you are hanging out with have a disparity of income. If you know one of your friends isn't raking in the six-figure salary you are, subtly offer to buy an extra round of drinks (or whatever) here and there. They will appreciate it, remember it, and get you back when they can.

Help others. Even if you are in the middle of getting some digits, always keep an eye out for your friends. For instance, when it is getting late and a female friend is leaving alone, help her hail a cab or wait outside with her until her hired car arrives. Or if a friend looks to have drunk too much, make sure they get home safely. Even better, send a follow-up text to your friends, making sure they made it home okay. Gestures like these will secure those digits too. Win-win!

MEN'S SOCIETY

MAINTENANCE ◆ DEPARTMENT

DON'T BE *THAT* GUY

You know, the guy who doesn't ask if anyone needs a drink before he goes to the bar to refresh his drink?

Conversation

Every man has different strengths, and the gift of gab may not be yours. Well, you're not alone. Especially at professional gatherings, you can't guarantee that everyone you meet, or find yourself in conversation with, is going to be your favorite person, interesting, or the easiest to talk to; however, following a few simple guidelines can help you not only survive the small talk, but also forge a genuine connection (and possibly charm the pants off everyone in the room—okay, let's not get crazy).

WHY DO WE (HAVE TO) CONVERSE?

To communicate, duh. But also to express ourselves, to learn, to persuade, to create an impression, to enjoy one another's company. A common mistake made especially by men is to view conversation as a kind of competition: Who is the most impressive? Who has the most intelligent opinion? Who will get all the attention? If you come at conversation with this attitude, you'll certainly make an impression: that of a boor (and a bore). At the other end of the spectrum, you may find conversing with others to be a chore or even beneath you, especially making small talk (again, boor/bore). Whatever your reason for entering into a conversation, be considerate.

CONSIDER THE SETTING

Perhaps it should go without saying, but different settings lend themselves to different kinds of conversation. That anecdote about your randy uncle might go down a storm at the bar, but may be less appropriate at dinner with your in-laws.

CONSIDER THE PERSON

Even more important than the setting is, of course, your audience. The nature of conversation will change with each new person you speak with; therefore, consider what sort of impression you want to make, and the nature of your relationship with that person, especially in professional settings. For example:

- Speaking to a superior may require you to be slightly deferential (i.e., be prepared to laugh at their bad jokes).

- A conversation with a potential client may also benefit from a bit of deference, but in this situation, more confidence from you may make them more at ease (i.e., at least pretend you know what you're talking about, even if you don't).

- With a subordinate, you may be the one setting the tone of the conversation (i.e., the "don't even try to be my bestie" tone).

MANSPLAINING

•

When a woman is explaining something, do you find yourself interrupting her with an "Actually, . . . " ? Then you're a mansplainer. Just like "manspreading" (page 137), "mansplaining" is a derogatory term that has recently entered our lexicon. What does it mean? Well, it is when a man speaks condescendingly to a woman, even though she has greater knowledge on the topic at hand, because, you know, he's a man (eye roll).

GUIDELINES FOR GOOD CONVERSATION

Whether you're at an office party or on a first date, here are a few general rules of conversation that will help you create a good impression and form a connection (even if it's fleeting).

Avoid sensitive topics. Even in relatively homogenous communities, you likely won't know everyone's beliefs in the room. Old-school etiquette dictates leaving politics and religion out of polite conversation. You don't want to sever a connection before it has a chance to grow, or inadvertently offend. Over the course of an evening, you may find you all share the same views, and then you can all go ballistic.

Keep it clean. Save the blue humor for your buddies. This isn't about being a prude, but rather waiting until you know the person across from you will appreciate a risqué comment, rather than be turned off.

Don't be a Debbie Downer. One of the biggest conversational pitfalls can be making negative or depressing comments and statements. Complaining can also make others feel uncomfortable. Both complaints and tales of woe seem to ask something of the

listener—whether it be a condolence or commiseration, or even unintentional problem-solving. That's not to say you need to be falsely cheery (no one likes that guy, either), but keeping your conversation light and positive can help grease the wheels of social interaction.

Don't gossip. Let's face it, we all enjoy a little gossip—it's human nature. It's also sometimes easier to bond with someone when speaking ill of others because what might feel like a sense of intimacy may quickly form between you. But beware: you don't know this person well enough to understand what their relationship is with that person, and you don't want to end up being the bad guy.

Be unselfish. Guess what? People love talking about themselves. So if worse comes to worst, be an active listener and ask lots of questions. And don't take it personally when your conversation partner doesn't reciprocate.

MEN'S SOCIETY

MAINTENANCE ◆ DEPARTMENT

DON'T BE *THAT GUY*

You know, the guy who is the blowhard who no one wants to talk to?

Use names. Using the other person's name is an excellent way to show that you are listening, engaged, and that your memory is intact. At least once in a conversation, use their name. Once is enough, John. Using their name too often, John, can seem a bit smarmy and off-putting, John.

Don't look at your phone. There's nothing ruder than someone looking at their phone while you're in the middle of a story, so only pull out your phone if it is literally blowing up in your pocket—like if it's on fire.

Be self-deprecating. A little self-deprecation can go a long way. Making fun of yourself a little (not too much) shows that you're funny and can help relax any situation.

Hospitality

If you've ever hosted a party yourself, you know the difference between a perfect guest, and, well, *that* guy. Whether dropping by for dinner or staying for the weekend, bring your guest A game and you're sure to be unforgettable (in a good way).

THE PARTY

Whether it's a dinner, a cocktail party, or even something less formal, there are a lot of moving parts to consider. And as a guest, you can help facilitate things, whether lending a hand or getting out of the way.

RSVP. Always RSVP, no matter how formal or informal the invitation is. Your host needs an accurate head count to have enough food and drinks on hand, which also means . . .

Don't guess about guests. If you want to bring a friend or two and the invitation is unclear about bringing guests, always ask the host if it will be okay to bring other people. In the same vein, if you were going to bring other people and now you're flying solo, let your host know this ahead of time.

Ask what you can bring. There may be something your host sorely needs, whether it's dessert or a bottle of vodka. Ask ahead of time, and if your host says, "Just yourself!" at least bring a bottle of wine. Never show up empty-handed, even if your closest friend has invited you over for a casual hangout.

Be (somewhat) fashionably late. No one wants to be the first one to arrive, but try to get there at a reasonable time out of repect for the host.

Offer help, then get out of the way. Your host may dearly need a hand, but that doesn't mean you should hover over their shoulder. Ask if they need anything or if you can help in anyway, and if the answer is no, phew, you can go have some fun.

Don't monopolize the host.
Maybe this is your best friend's shindig, but they have plenty of guests to tend to, not to mention they may be running back and forth to the kitchen to retrieve more food and drinks. Don't be offended if you only get a few minutes of face time. Say hello, ask if they need any help (see previous point), and do your own thing.

Clean up spills. There you are, gesticulating wildly with a full glass in your hand, and oops, a little spillage. Even if it's a small spill, make an effort to clean it up to be respectful of the host and their home.

MEN'S SOCIETY

MAINTENANCE ◆ DEPARTMENT

DON'T BE THAT GUY

You know, the guy who gets so drunk that he is referred to as the "drunk guy" by unacquainted partygoers for years to come?

Don't smoke. Unless there is a designated smoking area, don't light up a cigarette—or anything else (wink, wink)—without the host's permission. Even if you know your host has a pretty liberal attitude toward controlled substances, don't assume they're comfortable with that sort of thing at their own party (especially if you don't know the other guests well). And remember that your host may have trouble saying no, even if they want to.

Mingle. Though it can be tempting to stick to your circle of friends (seriously, what else do you have to talk about?), spread out and meet new people. Oftentimes, the parties considered to have been the most successful are the ones where you met new people.

THE LONG STAY
Filed under things that seemed like a good idea when planning them is the invitation for the long stay: "Of course it will be no trouble . . . no trouble at all." Wrong. Even for the most easygoing person, having a guest stay in your home can be trying. Here's how you can make your host's life easier while you're staying with them, and even remain friends.

Set dates and stick to them.
Even when staying with close
friends or family, you'll avoid
miscommunications and awkward
situations if you and your host are
clear on when you're arriving and
when you're leaving. You may
be the lowest-maintenance guest
in the world, but your host is still
changing the normal pattern of
their life for you. Don't assume that
showing up a day early—or worse,
staying a day longer—is kosher,
and don't put your host in the
position to have to say no.

Call or text before you arrive.
Give your host notice—thirty
minutes or so—before knocking
on the front door. Chances are
they're ready for you, but they
will appreciate the heads-up.

Gift something. Bring a bottle of
wine or a small gift when you arrive
for your stay, or pick something
up before you leave. It's a small
gesture, but a thoughtful one.

Be respectful of house rules. You
may not bother turning off the lights
when you leave a room at home, but
it's your host's house, and their rules.
Shoes on or off? Okay to drink red
wine on that white sofa? If your host
doesn't tell you specifically, ask, or
follow their example.

**Be a bathroom ninja (actually, it
might be easier to use the bathroom
at the gas station down the street).**
If you are sharing a bathroom with
others, make sure to leave it spotless
when you're done. That means put the
seat down (and flush it, for heaven's
sake), and wipe the sink down. Keep
your toothbrush and other essentials in
your dopp kit; don't take up valuable
sink space with your toiletries.

Ask before taking. Ask permission
before raiding the refrigerator (or
the bar). Don't assume that "make
yourself at home" means you can
help yourself to the last Hot Pocket.

Clear, wash, repeat. You may
have an aversion to doing your
dishes at home, but when staying
with someone else, don't leave
your dirty dishes sitting around.
Clear them and either wash them
or place them in the dishwasher.
If other people's dishes are also
sitting around, clear those too.

Go with the flow. The perfect
guest adapts to their host's style and
preferences. If your host is vegan,
maybe don't leave your meatball
parm in the refrigerator. Be mindful
of your host's religious beliefs, and
respectful of customs different from
your own. Remember, as a guest,
it's your job to fit in with their life,
not the other way around.

Feed yourself. Be as self-reliant as possible, especially when it comes to meals. If your host has a dinner idea, great! Otherwise, offer to pay for the groceries, shop for your own, or even better, show your gratitude by taking them out to dinner.

Give your host some space. Everyone needs some downtime, alone, so give your host some breathing room. For instance, if you typically stay up late, turn in early-ish so they don't feel obligated to stay up with you.

Leave your space just as (or better than) you found it. You should leave a pristine bedroom and bathroom every single day of your stay, not just when it's time to go. On your final day, strip the sheets and offer to wash them before leaving.

Send a thank-you note. It should be handwritten and sent within a few days of your stay. (See page 18 for more information on thank-you notes.)

SHOULD YOU OFFER TO COOK A MEAL FOR YOUR HOST?

•

Though the offer is generous and you mean well, using an unfamiliar kitchen can turn into a hassle for the host, especially if you need to constantly ask where different tools are stored.

Gifting

If you have a significant other who handles this, then cheers to you; otherwise, it's time to man up and master the art of giving cards and gifts—and possibly get more gifts in return (just kidding . . . kind of). Instant communication seems to have devalued the simple handwritten note or small thoughtful gift, but this only makes them all the more powerful and appreciated. Saying "thank you" in person, or in a text or email, or congratulating someone on their engagement in a social media post, just isn't the same.

> MEN'S SOCIETY
>
> MAINTENANCE ◆ DEPARTMENT
>
> ## DON'T BE *THAT GUY*
>
> *You know, the guy who makes the gift all about him instead of the intended recipient?*

WHEN TO GIVE CARDS AND GIFTS

There seem to be countless occasions in our lives that can be marked with celebrations or gifts. Concentrate on the big events and the most important people. (The asterisks mark occasions where only a card is necessary.)

- **Birthdays**
- **Holidays**
- **Weddings**
- **Engagement parties*** (a gift to celebrate an engagement is fine, though not necessarily expected)
- **Baby showers**
- **Religious events, such as a confirmation or bat/bar mitzvah*** (a monetary gift would be appreciated)
- **Graduations*** (as above, if you're close to the graduate)
- **New job or promotion***
- **New home***
- **During or after an illness***
- **Condolences***

WHEN TO SEND A THANK-YOU NOTE

Send a thank-you note whenever another person has extended themselves for you. Your note doesn't need to gush, or be longer than a handwritten line or two. When it comes to thank-you notes, it really is the sentiment and thought that count.

- **After receiving a gift** (birthday, wedding, baby shower, etc.)
- **To the host, after attending a formal gathering** (such as a dinner party)
- **After a job interview** (first send an email, followed by a handwritten note)
- **After an "informational" interview**
- **For a letter of recommendation**
- **After receiving an award**
- **After receiving a donation**
- **Whenever you feel appreciative**

HOW SOON SHOULD YOU SEND A NOTE?

•

Ideally, you should send a thank-you note within forty-eight hours of receiving the gift or attending an event, but there is no expiration on giving thanks, especially if you're not the most organized person.

About Men's Society

Every company has a backstory. This is ours:

Despite the name, we're not a cult, a bunch of do-gooders, or a club for cruising men; so apologies if you're reading this in a dark room expecting something a little racier. We are, however, a merry band of people creating fun, designed-focused, quality men's gifts.

We've had an exciting ride since we started all this in 2012. Like most businesses, it was born out of too much wine and some bold optimism. Our resignation from proper careers was followed by instant regret and severe panic about mortgage payments, before the realization set in, and we haven't been on holiday since.

Today, from our base in Lincolnshire (the undeniable center of the world), we supply some of the world's leading retailers with ranges of unique, British-made men's gifts. We travel to all corners of the globe—Tokyo, Brooklyn, Berlin, Shoreditch—to ensure that we stay current and on trend.

Our products are proudly hand-made in the UK by a lovely but terrifying team of tea-swigging ladies. Touch their biscuits and you die. Our kits are designed to be amusing and appealing, but, most importantly, they perform. Our all-natural beard oil is tried and tested and loved; our sneaker cleaning fluid has been developed alongside some of the country's best chemists to discover what really gets that dog shite off your Nikes.

Detail, design, and quality are at the heart of what we do, and pride, honesty, and creativity are at the heart of how we work.